"**M**AY ALL THE CURSES of the good Bishop Ernulphus light on the borrower-and-not-returner or upon the stealer of this book."

(Sir William Osler's inscription on the fly-leaf of his own copy of his *Textbook on the Principles and Practice of Medicine*)

CHILDREN'S EXPERIENCES IN ART

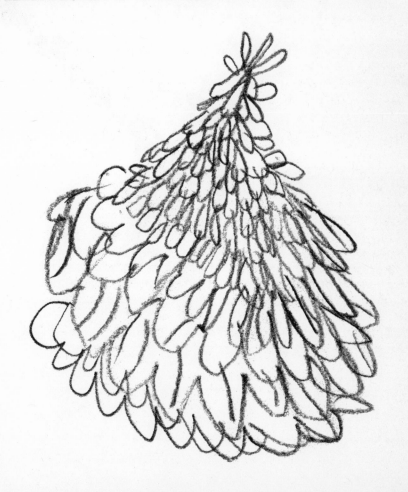

Children's Experiences in Art

Drawing and Painting

Pearl Greenberg

Photographs by Pearl and Murray Greenberg

Reinhold Publishing Corporation/New York

© 1966 Reinhold Publishing Corporation
All rights reserved
Printed in the United States of America
Library of Congress Catalog Card No. 66-11936

Designed by Emilio Squeglio
Type set by Lettick Typografic Inc.
Printed by New York Lithographing Corporation
Color printing by The Guinn Co.
Bound by Publishers Book Bindery, Inc.
Published by Reinhold Publishing Corporation
430 Park Avenue, New York

Dedicated to all of the children I have known through the years at Downtown Community School. Their interest in art knows no bounds and their joy in learning is an inspiration to all who work with them.

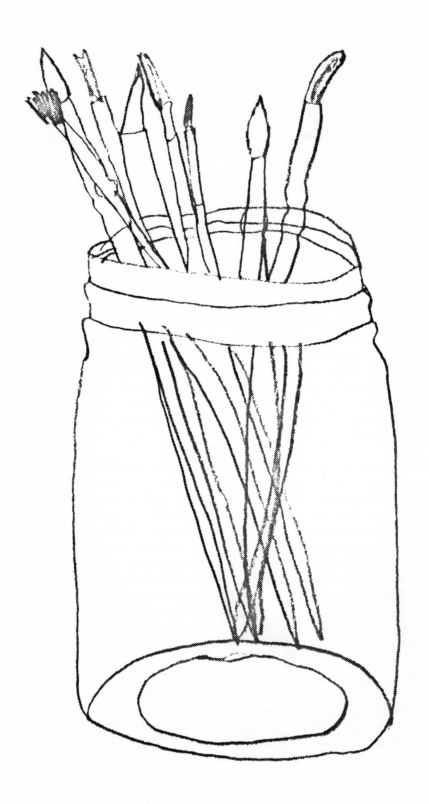

ACKNOWLEDGEMENTS

We take so much for granted as we grow toward maturity! It is not easy to know, among the maze of our experiences, which ones did and which ones did not affect our development. Who is to say? Of the people we have known, some-one hurriedly "passing through" might have given the right nod or look of under-standing, while another remained for a long time and yet offered little that helped one way or another.

Can a child know that something special may be happening, as you attempt to be his teacher, that he will never experience again? And, if he should realize it at some later date, will you ever know? When and if he ever does, he most likely will be years away from elementary school, and unable to remember your face or your name. Teaching is basically future-oriented, and we seldom see the changes in be-havior, the seeds of which we plant in each child.

The experiences that most profoundly help us to "become ourselves" happen at different times to different people. And what's more, they are differently sorted out, recognized and appreciated. I remember writing a "book" when I was eleven or twelve, based on a published series about teenagers and wild touring cars rac-ing at twenty miles an hour. Every time I was hung up for what to write next, I peeked back into a previous volume and combined situations to create my own masterwork. It was never finished. Prior to that, three or four poems had been published in the elementary school paper. A notebook full of others is still hidden in a carton underneath other memorabilia of childhood. It was not until I entered Cooper Union in September of 1945 that I became aware of myself as a person and, perhaps for the future, as an artist. The three happiest years of my life were spent here. Open to myself, I was soon able to relate with pleasure and anger to my peers — and we had a ball. Sydney Delevante was my drawing teacher, Leroy Buckingham taught English and Composition. The former taught me how to ex-press my innermost concerns through writing, the latter helped me to gain some understanding of the structure of language but allowed free reign in form. Here I also edited Pentracks, the literary magazine. So much happened, and so much mattered. We were concerned with the horrors of war, and the hopes of peace, with love and words and art. It was a total involvement which I shall always re-member. I cannot forget.

As for my teaching — I think I learned more from three years of assisting Lillian Lipsett, the art teacher at Downtown Community School, than I might have learned in several years of Education courses. To see this woman in action, bouncing from child to child, teaching in two rooms at the same time was extraordinary. She was a dynamo in action! And she was an inspiration. Later, when she decided that her energy had been consumed from such involvement, I was lucky enough to be at the right place at the right time, and was hired as the new art teacher.

A way of life opened up, a sense of caring about children and teaching, a desire to keep learning and to keep trying no matter what the odds. This was a total commitment which consumed the energy of everyone. My own involvement joined with that of many others. Among them were Norman Studer, Director of the Downtown Community School, and Irene Neurath, the Director of the Nursery School there, who were — and still are — the "leaders." They are very different from each other, yet each conveyed a sense of deep participation and caring, that teachers working with them caught and by which they, in turn, were inflamed. Certainly this redounded to the benefit of the children at the school, my own son included. We *did* care about each child, and we *did* try to do our very best for each one. This took time and energy above and beyond classroom or art room hours, and my husband soon became a much better cook than I will ever be because I'd come home so thoroughly enriched — and tired!

During these years others expanded my understanding of what teaching was all about. I attended New York University, studying with Chandler Montgomery and Hale Woodruff. They are dedicated teachers who respond magnificently to students who care about art and about teaching. At Teachers College, Columbia University, Raymond Patouillet and William J. Mahoney open up the world for those students who need more room to move about — to flex their muscles and their minds. In seeking excellent "models" for my own work, each of these great teachers has had something special to offer. Each has also helped me toward deeper self-understanding.

In gathering additional ideas and inspiration for my own teaching and philosophy I have often turned to the work of others. I should like to thank the publishers who have kindly given their permission to quote from some of these: G. P. Putnam & Sons for a passage from John Dewey's *Art as Experience;* Harvard University Press for passages from Jerome Bruner's *The Process of Education* and *On Knowing: Essays for the Left Hand;* Dover Publications for a passage from Hughes Mearns' *Creative Power;* Charles Scribners Sons for a passage from Martin Buber's *I and Thou.*

And to Sylvia Ashton-Warner, author of *Spinster,* and *Teacher,* published by Simon & Schuster, my sincere appreciation for exposing me to a philosophy about life and teaching which permeates all of my writing and my action in the classroom as well, for these cannot be separated.

I wish to acknowledge the kind permission granted by The Metropolitan Museum of Art for making photographs during field trips there with my classes. My special thanks to Irene Neurath and Grace Ilchuk for reading the manuscript, and for excellent suggestions leading toward clarification of important points. To Dori Watson a special round of applause for a very sensitive and superb job of editing. And most of all, my very special thanks to my husband who has been my photographer, and who has developed and printed hundreds of pictures, whose patience has too oft' been tried, but whose encouragement and confidence in me offered support without which I could not have managed through the years. And to our son, about to enter college, my appreciation for having wisely used the freedom we offered, and for his independent spirit and common sense.

CONTENTS

INTRODUCTION

What is that magic which makes someone a teacher?

> *... a person who is responsive and responded to.*
>
> *... a giver and receiver, whose standards expand and contract to meet the moment, aware of the need to set realistic goals.*
>
> *... a person who cherishes the wide range of individual differences and the limitless possibilities of imagination, who therefore leads each child toward developing his own "style" based on his unique responses to experiences.*

The effective teacher attempts to create an atmosphere that will lead toward a positive use of freedom by every individual child in a diverse group representing a wide range of experiences regarding the meaning and the value of freedom. The premise of this book is that as youngsters are helped to see, respond to, and develop a personal way of representing the world, the observing and involved adult also increases his awareness of the breadth and depth of creative possibilities — and is thus better able to stimulate the children.

We need constantly to learn more about art, about children, and about ourselves. We need to have experiences with art media for further insight into the process and problems involved, and to deepen our understanding of how these experiences can be redefined to meet the needs of the children we teach.

Noah drawing the coffee pot.

"ART IS PART OF ME."
— TEN-YEAR-OLD

14

 **PERSONAL
CONCERNS**

I guess I'll never overcome that feeling of worry the very first day of school. Waiting for the children to come into the art room — well, I feel the way an actor feels on opening night. I feel something of the composer's anticipation as he strains to hear the opening notes of his latest work being presented before a waiting audience for the first time.

During the summer months all of us, teachers and children alike, developed a different rhythm for our daily living. Now we come together once again and it's time to regain that special rhythm of the school year. I wonder if I'll be able to do it. I wonder, too, how different the children will be. They are, all of them, only a few months older, and yet a whole grade ahead. They arrive — the familiar faces, and also some new ones. They are all alert and waiting for magic to take place. A few are missing — and missed. From Alissa, this note: "Goodbye to our rainy Thursdays, for I shall not return. Love, Alissa." It had rained nearly every Thursday morning that year. Which will be the rainy day this year, I wonder?

In they come. Last year's six-year-olds holding themselves straight and tall as they imagine seven-year-olds should. We try to adjust to this new change in status. We seek for the new rhythm that will "fit." As they leave, Kappy looks up at me, overflowing with wisdom: "Mrs. Greenberg, you've grown since last spring!" "Have I, Kappy? That's good. And so have you!" He beams and walks on out holding the hand of a new boy whose name I must learn next time. Will I learn the new names quickly?

Five minutes for cleaning up the room. Another group arrives. We see a beautiful film on color. I'm suddenly struck by the fact that these little fourth-graders might assume that they can afford to be as free with paint as the film shows, using big pools of color to indicate the variety one can create from red, yellow and blue. We discuss parts of the film, and as I start to say something about the copious use of paint, Jaime raises his hand.

> *"Well, the people who made the movie use lots of paint because they're making the movie to make money, so it's O.K. if they spend a little more money since they know they'll make money and they need to do a good job to make even more money. But we aren't trying to make money so we need to be careful about how much we use, because we can't spend as much as they can — since they are making money on the movie!"*

All in one breath, Jaime delivers our economics lesson for the day! As he speaks, murmurs of agreement from his classmates show that they understand. The rest of our time together flies by. We mix colors and paint. In addition to provoking the comments on economics, the film has been quite an inspiration.

The first meetings pass. The new rhythm is slowly coming through to me. As I look at some of the paintings and drawings, as I react to the individual children, I feel to a degree that I belong again. But still, I am, in the words of Thoreau, "stepping to the tune of a different drummer." It takes time to become fully involved. Looking back as a year progresses I realize that we end each school year full to the brim of involvement; we return to each new semester refreshed, ready for the new beginning that will lead toward that height of involvement once again. Each new school year is an opportunity for rebirth. Each may add to our fund of knowledge and provide fresh opportunities for the experiment and experience that will lead to new insight and understanding. Each is a chance to become — and remain — a little more aware.

All of these experiences are sifted through us. Some of them are internalized and help us to become more able teachers. We are in great part formed and sensitized by those we teach. As well as being ourselves, we are shaped by the sum of our experiences over the years. But it's good to know that each year can also stand alone, be worthy of itself, and then be added on to all those that have passed. This accumulation of experiences makes me a different person at the start of each school year.

How much easier it seems for our first graders to become second graders after the summer solstice! They, too, are moving into new experiences. They, too, must find the new rhythm for school, for independence, for cooperation, for meeting and attempting to solve so many new problems, as well as overcoming what might have been a summer of less than successful experiences.

> *"Mrs. Greenberg, I lost all my talent this summer! The art teacher at camp said we had to draw and paint exactly what he wanted. We couldn't do anything else!" This from Tommy, a ten-year-old who had thrived on his joyous experiences in art during the school year.*

Parents, too, must face each new year, learning as time passes to allow the child increasingly to become a separate person, living as an individual outside of the home and as part of a group of children in a situation in which the teacher becomes the guiding light. Parents are the child's first teachers from the very start of his life. It is certainly not easy to adjust to sharing this child with strangers, forfeiting something of the control and influence over him. But this, too, is part of the rhythm of living and growing.

16

There are so many experiences in art class that await the child. Creating, seeing and displaying finished work, posing for classmates are all part of it. We hope that these moments are full of self-expression, learning, and delight for every child from the beginning discussion to "clean-up" at the end. Here (upper left), David, age ten, explores a new medium. He is working with felt tipped pens on a sheet of plastic. Celeste is shown (upper right) as she posed for her classmates. Some of their drawings of her appear on page 53. Six-year-old Madeline proudly holds up her finished work (below). She used tempera mixed with soap flakes and applied to a plastic sheet for her painting.

Susan 7th

The two drawings of trees on this page record the impressions of children of different ages. Adam, seven, drew what he "knew" trees looked like. Susan, twelve, recorded what she observed of a specific tree.

In their art children show us how they change and grow. From month to month, year to year, the child records his vision of the world. At any point, we know the vision will further mature and broaden, but each statement in painting or drawing tells us how far along he has already come in the wonderful growing process. We rejoice in his present control, his awareness and observation of things about him, his mastery of techniques, and his insights into himself and others. At the same time, we subtly and gently urge him toward the greater command and understanding that will be his tomorrow. What a challenge — and responsibility!

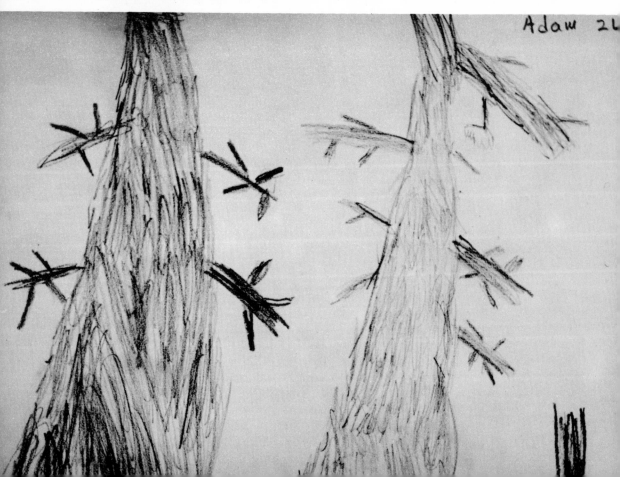

Adam 2L

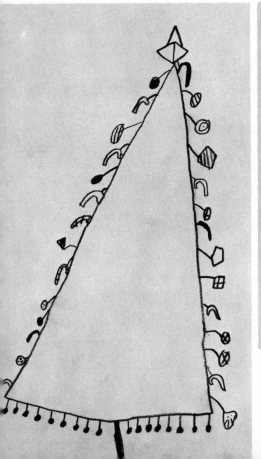

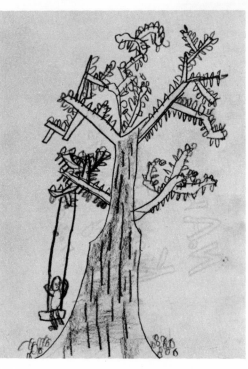

Tony is obviously pleased with his painting.

"ART IS SOMETHING YOU HAVE A TEMPTATION TO DO."
— NINE-YEAR-OLD

 **FOUNDATIONS
FOR LEARNING**

It is hoped that this book will be a temptation for you — a temptation to explore, via photographs and words, children's responses to art and to life through their eyes, hands, and minds.

Whatever our area of specialization, as teachers our work involves being and remaining aware, flexible, open to experimentation, questioning, and finding new directions. In fact, these are the very traits we hope to develop in the children we attempt to teach. Whether we work with "normal" children or with children in need of special attention, the sense of being deeply involved and caring enough sometimes works that bit of magic that turns education into a fascinating adventure.

Children are not simply "units." They are complex beings, made increasingly more complex by each new experience. Yet, with all the complexity, they are at every stage whole and integrated individuals. It is the whole self that is experiencing and categorizing, organizing a dazzling amount of material at a very rapid pace — in a sense forming itself (or being formed) out of life and learning. And it is the whole self that responds to the many and diverse demands of every waking moment.

Communication is far more intricate and complicated than simply expressing an idea in terms of the verbal symbols we call words, and being understood and answered in like manner. It reaches into much more subtle realms where often there are no words at all to parallel what is being said. And yet communication is taking place. What greater joy is there when, as a child, you find that you can look at something and then note it down on paper in the form of a picture, a poem, or a musical composition? Suddenly you are able to communicate in another, and sometimes richer language than of words. What is more, people understand — and respond!

Six-year-olds apply themselves to the serious business of working with brushes and paints.

Eugene, age twelve, studies his subject carefully. His finished drawing of a tree will be more "realistic" than the drawing to the right.

A seven-year-old's drawing of a tree.

So much can be said with a few flowing lines. Some do this best in dance, poetry, or in prose. For some, the lines may be "spoken" best using a guitar or a clarinet. For others, the only way to communicate, beyond the use of words, is with pencil, charcoal, or brush and paint.

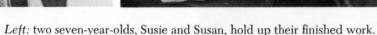

Left: two seven-year-olds, Susie and Susan, hold up their finished work.

The variations and combinations of creative output are great. To teach is to know this. To be a successful teacher is to recognize the precious differences and aptitudes of every child. While some are more highly endowed than others, each child should have the opportunity to explore the numerous means of expression under the guidance of adults well versed in the creative arts process. Every child should have the chance to try to explore and discover the many different means of expression, because among them he may find a way of "talking" — of expressing himself.

Each child is unique. Each is special. And the reaching out to guide and help each child to discover his own special potential and expressiveness is the function of the teacher. The learning and creative process then prompts the teacher to thrust him outward toward some horizon experience. The child will follow, challenging, questioning, learning, and remain open-ended in his expectations, eager to learn of the breadth and depth of living. A child will quickly learn to express what is real for him. And the teacher, leading, at the same time becomes increasingly aware of the value and wonder of the child's point of view.

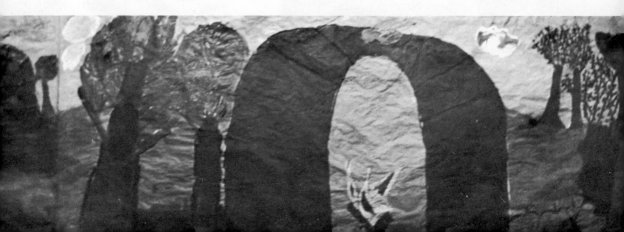

The teacher "sets the stage" for learning.

Posing problems and asking questions we try to help children "think" about possible answers. Having had many previous experiences we tend to ask questions for which we have ready answers and often we are looking for the one or two answers we consider "right." *We* need to be open to answers which are different and which are unique. *We* need to allow children time to think, to mull over a question, rather than expect quick responses that require only shallow thinking. *We* need to help those who need extra time, and at the same time we must avoid stifling those who are able to respond quickly.

Yes, this does use valuable "doing" time. But this too, is an important part of learning. Whether in the art studio or the classroom, the discussion and the thinking are important if the work experience is to be of any value.

Six- and seven-year-olds tend to fidget after a few minutes of discussion, but can accept a combination of talk and visual aid materials as motivation for using art media. If "listening" and "thinking" become part of the motivation at the start, they will not balk at the continuation, and on occasion, even the extension of such discussion. This is the groundwork for the discussions on art and artists, that become an important part of the curriculum for middle and upper graders.

When the teacher demonstrates a technique, she makes some remarks about the process, suggests and shows alternatives, and points out that there may be a number of ways in which the medium can be used. She offers the children an opportunity to question and to suggest still other possible ways of working. This helps her to find out whether they are able to understand the principles or concepts involved. She tries always to make the assignment in terms that further allow experiences rather than saying, "This is it, now you do it in just this way."

Thirteen-year-olds are engrossed in sketching out-of-doors.

In the art room seven-year-olds receive some guidance.

Dick asked for some black paint and then found a short cut for getting it quickly.

Children need to feel at ease, yet know that they must work within a certain acceptable framework of discipline. They need to know that success is possible and that the teacher is there for support at moments of failure. They need to know that what they produce or create is appreciated, and that criticism is meant to help them to improve.

Third-graders looking at a portfolio of paintings.

Children need opportunities to see their work and the work of their peers in order to learn to understand and appreciate differences as well as similarities. From this, they will learn that we each have different ways of seeing and responding to the world in which we live, as well as similar reactions to some of our experiences.

28

Creating the proper atmosphere and "spirit" for learning is a very important part of the teacher's role. Before beginning to work on this occasion, we had a short "meeting" session, everyone sitting around a large table. This would be a painting time in which the children were free to paint as they desired. If anyone had an idea that he wanted to talk over with me, that was fine. Any who felt they just couldn't think of something really interesting to do were free to discuss the problem with me. I had two small groups in need of my individual assistance. The rest of the class went to the painting area and immediately set to work.

The children who felt they "just couldn't think of anything" were asked to have a quiet talk with each other for a few minutes while I attempted to help those who felt they had a good idea but needed some advice. I gave the former group some crayons and paper to use in addition to suggesting that they talk quietly together. When I returned to their table, two had already decided to start their paintings and two felt there was just nothing they cared to paint. But they did ask, "May we continue drawing?" and, "Where are the cray-pas?"

Many of us probably have known at least one teacher who had a very special influence which we cherish to this day. It is likely that we were not really aware of this special "touch" at the time, but see it in retrospect as having been the influence that led us in a desired direction. On the other hand, there are numerous cases when a child was told: "You can't work in art because you're not staying within the lines when you color." or: "Don't sing anymore, you're a listener." or: "You can't paint for a week because you spilled the blue paint into the green." Leading children to learn and inspiring them to want to learn is never accomplished successfully through negatives.

Nine-year-olds painting during a "free" period.

Design in mixed media by a ten-year-old.

Our work constantly revolves around the elements of line, color, texture, form and space. Therefore, plastic, visual, tactile, and verbal expressions are all involved as motivating factors in developing an art experience. All of these are methods of communication. They are interrelated, and are used in different degrees as factors in learning.

If we believe that art experiences should allow children to think for themselves, to experiment and explore, while building onto an ever growing base of technical knowledge, then we need to concern ourselves with the types of motivation that stimulate children toward such learning.

We need to consider the validity of open-ended art experiences, and a topic-oriented curricula. We must teach within a framework establishing situations that lead toward further growth rather than to a dead end, asking questions and encouraging the many possible ways to look for the answers.

The six-year-olds here are working with felt-tipped markers.

the

But to be

It is not our aim to develop artists when working with young children. We are concerned with art as a means for expanding the child's awareness and ability to communicate. We are interested in helping teachers to understand and accept the validity of art experiences in the curriculum. There is great benefit to be derived if the child may learn to personally enjoy art. And it is imperative that all adults involved with children realize that art is one of the important ways in which children can express themselves as individuals.

Learning based on real and concrete experience has meaning. Seeing, hearing, touching, lifting, smelling, tasting, manipulating — all of these add to and enrich the learning process. So often, children find their most meaningful expression in the world of creativity and through the arts.

Eight- and nine-year-olds enjoy an outing as part of the art curriculum.

Teachers at an art workshop run by the author.

A philosophy does not evolve overnight.

As we learn more about ourselves, about art, and about children, we begin to see connections, we begin to discover what the learning and creative processes are all about. As we have personal experiences with art media we gain further insight into the methods and the problems. We reach some understanding of how these experiences might be redefined for the children in our classrooms.

This discovery of the depth and the challenge of teaching is not a case of doing something once and feeling one has had an adequate experience. Once is only an introduction — the tasting of a delicious tidbit that becomes an incentive for more.

Sixth-graders visit The Metropolitan Museum of Art as part of their study of China and India.

It is our desire to help children realize that art is an integral part of life, that it has been a central means of expression since prehistoric days when man depicted familiar animals on cave walls and ceilings. If children are exposed to a wide range of media as used by other cultures as well as our own, art becomes truly alive for them. Although it continues to be very personal as an experience, art also opens the door to developing understanding and an appreciation of the past and the ever changing present.

Art does not come with an answer book. There are many possible solutions to any one problem. There are many choices one can make in creating a personal statement. There is no substitute for personal experiences with the materials of art.

Facing a blank piece of paper with a brush or pencil in hand, we gain insight into the problems of getting started — of making the first mark where no one has made a mark before. We find that the blank paper itself is a little intimidating.

Rachel and Laura begin their paintings together.

We face frustrations when solutions to art problems do not come easily even after a good start. But there is pleasure in arriving at the best solution that, in turn, removes doubt that the creative power in each of us can be positively stimulated by successful experiences in art.

The child who says "I can't" has been taught to believe that he really can't, and he has learned this lesson well. It takes time for children to differentiate between positive and negative learning. When he feels that he can't, when he hears adults say that he can't, when there is no counteracting force to help him try and to show him that he can, the pattern is set. But sometimes the very smallest bit of appreciation — a sign that you care and want to help — will give such a child the courage to try once again.

Such a child cannot always be helped by following all the rules and regulations one learns about in teacher education. For example: a six-year-old, after working with clay, asked for a crayon and paper to draw a person. He held these in his left hand and followed me around, talking about how he wanted to draw, went to the table to start, and then sat and meditated. "I want to do it but I can't. It won't look real." The rest of his class finished their clay work and he joined them in clean-up activities. During the following art time the same thing happened again. He did not want any suggestions; he told me that he knew what a person looked like, but he was still not willing to make a first mark on his paper. Others in the class needed some assistance, but he kept following close behind me. Then, I sat down with him and said, "Why don't you show me what you *can't* draw, and then I'll be able to help you!" He looked astonished at this suggestion. "Do you mean it? Show you what I can't draw? that sounds silly." "Well, unless you do, I won't know how to help!" Seeing that I was not fooling even though it was, admittedly, a strange request, he went to his table, sat down, and drew a man. And it was a fine drawing, using the kinds of symbols one reads about in relation to children's drawings! He was not satisfied with his picture because he could do other things far advanced for a six-year-old. But this helped to get him drawing people; he brought new drawings to me the following week and went on from there.

Some children show different "selves" at different times or places. A student teacher in our art room spoke of Stephen to the assistant teacher in his classroom, "What a wonderful boy! Seems to get involved with his work, really cares, tries hard, respects tools, works with others." The classroom assistant was astounded. "Him? He's one of the worst kids in the class! Always in trouble, bothers the others, can't sit still. How can you say such nice things about him?" One atmosphere allowed Stephen to function well; the other brought out the worst in him. When such differences in a child's behavior appear, it is important for teachers to cooperate, to see if there is some way — or many ways — to help him feel at ease in any situation.

When there are specialists in a school, it is extremely important that lines of communication between the grade teacher and the special-subject teachers remain open. Thus it is possible to note how different children respond in a variety of situations. It is also wise to limit the number of such people very young children meet in a day. I'm reminded of a six-year-old who became confused when there were three adults he could turn to in the art studio (myself and two student teachers). Finally, placing his hands on his hips he said, "Well, who's the boss around here, anyhow?"

Nina, age seven, is deeply engrossed in her work.

"ART IS WORKING WITH YOUR HANDS AS WELL AS YOUR MIND."
— ELEVEN-YEAR-OLD

3 TIME FOR ART

When we become involved in something interesting, time is always too short. Almost as soon as we start it is time to stop. How often we hear children ask: "What? Time to stop already? But we just started!" For many children art time is as a ten-year-old boy described it, "a special opportunity to be together; other school work keeps us separate."

Although time for art is scheduled in the school day, there should be other moments when children may feel free to enjoy painting or drawing. They may find this "extra time" in the art room during recess, at noon or after school. This offers opportunities for children to break through the age barriers too often set by being divided into set age-grade levels. They see a wider range of working methods and materials, and seem to widen their own horizon in trying new approaches. We need to consider giving such experiences to many more children. By keeping children in units based on age, we harness some who might flourish in mixed age groupings.

Concentration is one key to the productive use of any learning periods. The ability to become involved in any given type of experience varies, depending upon many factors. Young children have a short attention span, compared to that of nine- or ten-year-olds. And yet, there are times when a four-year-old will become so involved that he can use blocks or crayons for half a morning.

It is not always easy to predict how long a group of children should, or will remain interested in a given art medium. Some six-year-olds will work on as many as three paintings in a fifty minute art session; others become so fully involved that they ask for more time to complete the painting when the period has come to an end.

We live within the framework of a society that functions by the clock; there are many things which must be accomplished during any given day. The result too often is that we tend to become far more concerned about "things" and too little with "ideas." How helpful it would be if we could find some compromise that would allow flexibility, at the same time functioning within the schedules and time limitations set by the requirements of daily living.

The child who gives up quickly, who seems frustrated even before applying that first paint stroke to paper needs the teacher's special attention. He needs encouragement to bolster him up and help him over the barrier of fear that he will fail. It is not easy to be successful if you are worried about failing. Even a small measure of success will be enough to make it possible for many children to forge ahead and to feel better about themselves and what they create. A child who can concentrate on what he is doing becomes so involved that time does seem to fly by. He may have moments of frustration, but feels secure enough to seek the solution that is "right" for him.

"People Rushing" is the title a seven-year-old gave his painting.

The special opportunity to finish an important painting.

As children grow they become more aware of time; they learn that limits are set by planning work to occupy a certain time, that time must be allotted for returning materials to the right boxes and cabinets. Brushes need to be washed really clean so the next group will find them in a condition worthy of use. But in addition to learning the disciplined use of time they also need the experience of knowing that there are opportunities for some extra work time for a "worthy cause" — for finishing a cherished painting while the spirit is still high.

Younger children work quickly, and seem to be finished almost before they start. As they grow older and the ability to concentrate increases, they need to have the pleasure of finishing their work without being pressured to start something new. And then, too, time is needed for looking at the work of their peers while all are full of the desire to share experiences.

We all need some moments when we are allowed to make a statement without an audience asking for an explanation or interpretation. The "artist" in each of us demands this. For some, the statement is verbal — in poetry or prose. For others, it is made in paint, with clay, in music, or the dance. We must not forget how to communicate with ourselves although our efforts seem most often to be directed toward communication with others, and even here we cannot always succeed.

As teachers we need to exert caution in attempting to bring up a breed of over-integrated children who do not learn enough about themselves in their zeal to be part of everything about them. There is so little opportunity for self-searching. Through the arts it becomes possible to bring forth responses which may have been lying dormant for too long. Here alone lies an opportunity for personal expression without negating the need for communication with others. Perhaps this is one way to help ourselves, as well as those we teach, to rediscover the poetry in life.

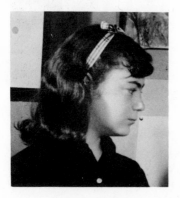

How often does a child have a quiet time for thinking, off and alone, deep in his own world?

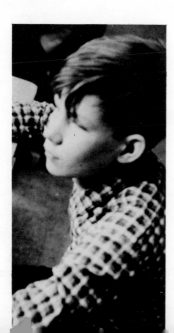

43

Even when working close by another person it is possible to become fully engrossed in one's own work. Children learn to respect each individual's need for quiet moments for concentration (above). They also enjoy moments of controversial, thought-provoking discussion. Furiously moving marker or whatever drawing tool is at hand, they make an important point (below).

One of the major goals of any teacher is to help each child approach new experiences with a minimum of fear and with enough of a sense of security to help him overcome minor frustrations and learn to cope with problems that might otherwise become real roadblocks. Being available at just the right moment, when a smile or a nod of approval is needed, often does much more to help a child than words-words-words.

If you have ever visited a classroom or art room where the teacher just never seemed to stop talking, you remember how difficult it was for children to concentrate on their work. We can't expect complete silence. This is often the only opportunity children have for talking to each other freely and exchanging ideas. In addition there are often street noises or hall noises close by, but it is possible for most people to block out these sounds. The teacher who compulsively talks, whose remarks are always directed to the entire class, who cannot communicate on a one-to-one basis with the child she needs to talk to, but who must make pronouncements for all, creates a work-defeating atmosphere. Concentration in such an atmosphere is almost impossible. Teachers often expect long periods of silence from children; they need to set an example by their own disciplined behavior as well. Talking constantly at children cannot be equated with good teaching. Nor does a room where children do art work in complete silence indicate that any real learning is going on. There is a difference between meaningless noise and the sounds produced by work which are part of the excitement of learning and doing.

In attempting to evolve an atmosphere that will allow creativity to flourish we must remain aware of the need to develop integrated human beings. We offer exposure to many and varied experiences, but we also attempt to show connections so that education does not consist of bits and pieces of learning. We believe that certain experiences should be had by all, but then we must allow a child the privilege of not doing some things, if he so chooses on occasion. For at some point in growing up, a child deserves the right to this freedom. This does not mean that we negate the need for children to take part in all aspects of school life, but that we do respect their occasional right to be alone, to be "out of things" at times. Otherwise we set up a regimented conformity that can be nothing less than stifling.

To a great extent the atmosphere that will help each child to express himself and to learn is created by the teacher who cares. How comforting to have the teacher give him her attention for a few minutes; she listens to a story or tries to help solve the immediate problem. Then she moves on, quietly, to offer help to the next child.

Art experiences offer children the opportunity to make important personal statements. As they grow, children are building on these statements, making choices, learning the "language" of art, solving problems, and acquiring techniques. We assume there is an inter-action between all these areas of expansion that is leading toward individual depth in learning. We offer children art media for esthetic and kinesthetic experiences and use numerous methods of motivation. The major method to stimulate learning seems to be verbal, with asking questions as the initial approach toward inspiring responses. Visual materials enhance such a motivational method. Films, reproductions, prints, teacher-made materials, and the children themselves, or other "models" which meet the immediate need, are used.

When drawing from the model, older students spend a moment of careful looking before putting pencil to paper. They understand the need to observe the pose and do some advance planning to consider how and where to make that first important mark on the paper.

Children of different ages enjoy an art session together after school.

Experiences do not take place in a void; there is a "before," a "during," and an "after." Having an experience once is only the bare beginning. Dr. Bruner, in *The Process of Education*, states, "A curriculum as it develops should revisit basic ideas repeatedly, building upon them until the student has grasped the full formal apparatus that goes with them."

Too often "once is always," and learning remains superficial. Art seems to suffer from this approach in many an elementary classroom and art studio. Rather than going into depth in drawing or painting experiences, some teachers seem to think that they must offer children a new and different technique or art medium every day. This leads to shallow experiences, allowing no real opportunity for a second chance to improve, or even for a successful beginning with a specific assignment (drawing a person, for example). Spending more than one or two art periods drawing people seems the only natural way to inspire children to look at and really see themselves and others, and to learn to use the tools and techniques of drawing. A youngster learning how to play a musical instrument, even a simple recorder, must practice daily in order to avoid sour notes. This is also true with drawing. By constantly changing art media it is as though we decide that instead of practicing steadily on his recorder, the child must today play the piano, tomorrow the clarinet, the following day the drums, and so on.

This is a plea for avoiding gimmicks and for spending more time than we now do with the basic art media, offering a broad range of experiences on which an excellent art program can be built. While appearing to limit, we can actually expand what children learn. Within any medium there are many possible variations on a theme — so many ways in which children can work while sustaining interest on a high level. Exploring these will impart unity and meaning to the experiences; constantly changing for the novelty of change results in an incoherent and superficial program.

We don't need a mountain of supplies in order to offer children the joy of discovering the unknown for themselves. The materials for drawing, painting, printing, sculpture, pottery, and constructions are basic and are available in nearly every school. Too often lack of "elegant" supplies is used as the excuse for a poor art curriculum. If the basic art media are available, the aware teacher will make good use of them. She will introduce each slowly, allowing children the pleasure of savouring each experience fully, gradually demonstrating new ways of working as each child seems ready to move on. She does not overwhelm them by offering too many choices, but seeks to bring out the richness and range of possibilities each medium offers.

Eli drawing a city scene.

"DRAWING IS A PICTURE OF SOMETHING
IN YOUR MIND PUT DOWN ON PAPER."
— ELEVEN-YEAR-OLD

 **DRAWING**

Observe a group of children sketching each other and you will hear exclamations of amazement when they see themselves from different views — many for the first time. We normally see ourselves full-face; but others see us from a variety of angles and in many moods and positions — moving about, happy or sad, slumping in our seats, dancing gaily, falling to the gym floor, tired and breathing heavily. Children notice these things about each other. Given the opportunity to draw or paint people they often show great insight.

In some drawing periods we have used "posed" models — usually one of the children in the class. This may be done from the first grade right on up through the eighth. While the six-year-old will spend more time looking at his drawing paper than at the posed model, he begins to get the idea about other ways of drawing. At the same time, he is free to continue to use the symbols with which he has become comfortable. Gradually, young children do spend more time looking and really trying to see the model; by the second or third grade, many find pleasure in being able to capture even the semblance of a likeness to the child posing.

Drawing with soft lead pencils or crayons, these first-graders spend more time looking down at their papers than at the model, who reminded them that he was posing with hand on hips. "We know, we know!" was their reply. And they did know, as can be seen in the three drawings above.

For drawing we have used soft lead pencils, crayons (oil base and wax), felt tip markers, charcoal, pastels, India inks, and chalks. These media are used individually, any one offering an excellent opportunity for drawing. "Mixed," they combine to create unusual textures and colors.

Paper is manufactured in 9 x 12, 12 x 18, and 18 x 24 inch standard sizes. Children are pleased to find that the sheets on which they may work are changed at times. The standard paper may be cut so that there are an even greater number of choices available. Sometimes a drawing or painting idea works best on a 12 x 15 or 15 x 19 inch paper. Perhaps a long strip, 5 x 18, is needed; this means by cutting a larger paper down it will give us the strip and leave another piece of paper which will be the right shape for someone else to use. Cut a number of papers at one time and allow the children to decide which shape or size is right for the work at hand.

The student posing enjoys a new experience when shown the results of sitting in one position for twenty minutes or more! Here, sixth-graders each saw the model from a similar angle and interpreted the pose in his own individual "style."

Since many children paint themselves full-face, as they see themselves, seeing sketches done of them by others, as well as looking and drawing others in turn, helps them to see and understand facial and bone structure. Older students have the interest and patience to do long studies as well as enjoying doing quick sketches. Also, they are keenly interested in the differences in appearance among themselves as well as other children of different ages. One excellent way of giving them the opportunity to observe and draw others is to allow them to visit classrooms where two or three can sketch without disturbing the younger children at work. Another time they might observe and sketch these same children at play out-of-doors.

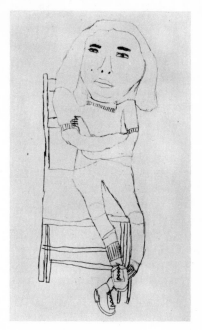

Children can portray a variety of feelings and actions. For the few who say "I can't," trying out the pose helps them to feel at ease and familiar with the body movement they want to show. Sometimes a classmate will accommodatingly model for a few minutes.

When asked to draw themselves in a pose or to do self portraits, some children insist, quite rightly, they just don't know what they look like. If a large mirror is available this problem is soon solved. They take long looks, mimic, check to see eye color, hair length, and are reassured about where to place their features.

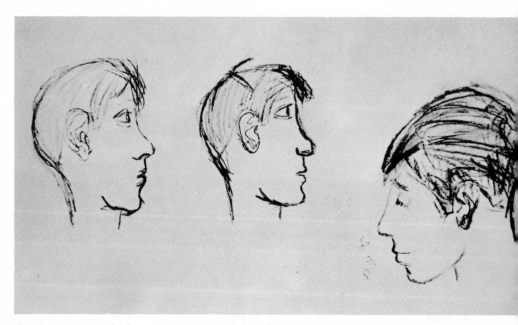

Ken drew Peter and Chris, using a soft lead pencil.

By posing for each other, children learn more about themselves as well. In small groups they can look at the results and, with the teacher's help, learn to develop critical thinking. When they understand that each new drawing, and the advice of peers and teachers, will help them to improve, they worry less about petty reactions and losing friends who might be insulted! They discover the delight in observing things carefully. As an eleven-year-old put it, "When you *have* to look at something, you suddenly really see it!"

A ten-year-old shows his dad relaxing — slippers and all.

Homework assignments for those in the middle and higher grades might include drawing members of the family. Here, children may be asked to show people relaxing, working, or doing things together as a family. They may be asked to observe and sketch something typical about someone at home. Such assignments interest parents and siblings. This is one special way in which art is brought to the home and is also of value as a learning experience. The final result need not always be one "finished" drawing. It may consist of a number of studies. In attempting to solve a particular problem in observing their models, these students whose work appears below did many quick drawings on a single sheet of paper.

Occasionally an adult will pose for the children.

This points up how different we look to each one in the class, and relaxes those who might worry when drawing their peers for fear of not achieving an "exact" likeness. Our aim is to observe the combination of lines, forms, and textures that makes us each look the way we do.

When working from the posed figure, it is interesting to look at the model from many points of view. The sketches on the right were made from the front, side, and back. The same piece of paper was used for two views in each case. Drawing the same subject from a number of angles gives the child a better understanding of the form. He can make comparisons between his several sketches, note where both the observation and drawing were more effective, and see where to make improvements next time.

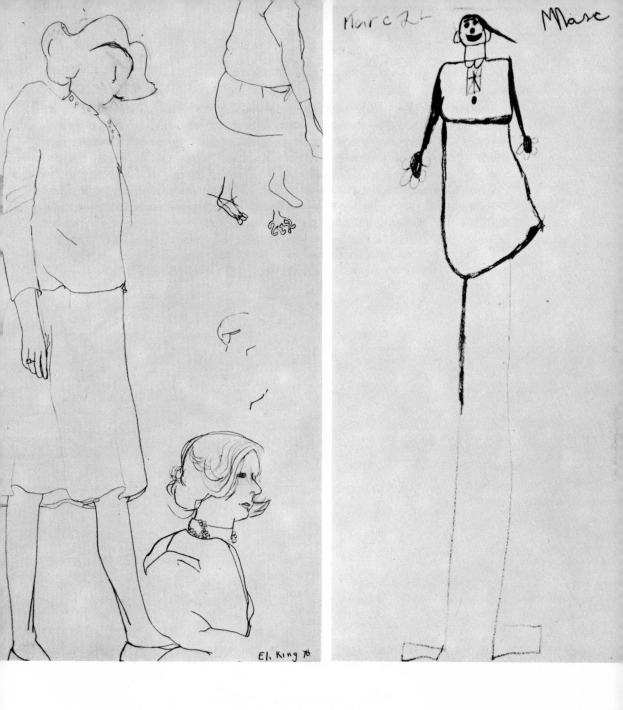

Looking at the model from a fresh and unusual angle — from above or below, for example — invites children to rely even more on observation. They not only draw the figure, but also show the effect of distortion on it from the different point of view. Eli, age twelve, and Marc, seven, each chose to sketch the model as she stood on a table, placing the drawing pad at her feet. They looked up at the model instead of seeing her at eye level, thereby achieving these interesting drawings. (These were not done at the same time; each child worked with his own classmates.)

Contour drawing, which is caressing the outside of a shape with the eye as the pencil is moved along by the hand on the drawing paper, is one of the most effective ways to sharpen the powers of observation. Children and adults alike are shocked at first when confronted with the results of such a limitation — keeping to a steady line rather then using sketching strokes, and looking at the subject rather than at the paper. At first they feel it can't be done. Then, after trying it a few times, suddenly they are freed from the worry of achieving a realistic likeness, and find they can capture the feeling **and form** with ease.

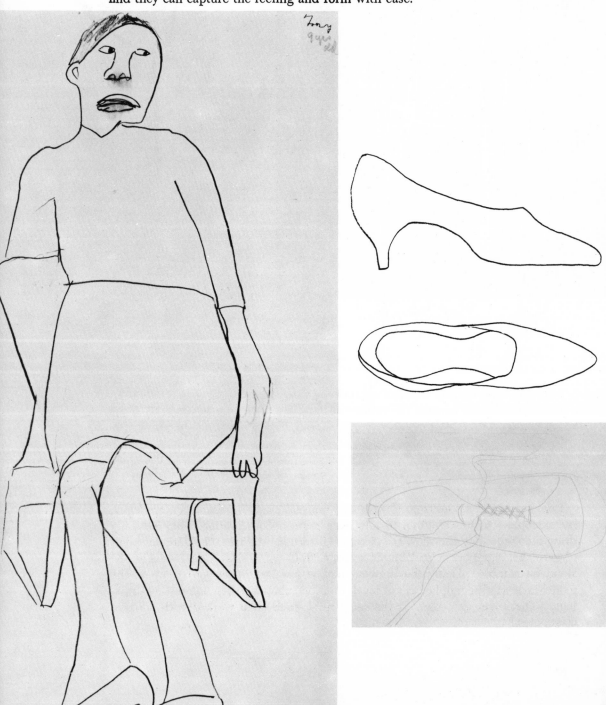

Having achieved the freedom contour drawing gives, it is easier to attempt a "realistic" drawing because the contour technique brings a greater mastery of the drawing tool. Whether drawing a person, an ink bottle, coffee pot, or plant, using the contour method, especially from about the age of ten on, loosens a child's drawing technique, helps him to really see what he might otherwise only casually observe, and frees him to re-arrange the appearance of a form to suit the space he plans for it.

The experience of contour drawing can be naturally followed by adapting it to a number of different drawing techniques. In the drawing on the right, a thirteen-year-old has used crayon to achieve quick textural gestures combined with fine and direct linear movement. Another possibility is to produce a "negative image" drawing by using white chalk on black paper, as in the drawing on the left. Since this is the reverse of what drawings usually look like, the lines take on a greater vividness and inspire new interest.

59

Although contour drawing as such was not introduced to second graders, in an instance illustrated on these two pages a child created a series of four drawings that closely approach the contour technique. Sometimes just encouraging children to look carefully at something will tempt them to "see with their pencil."

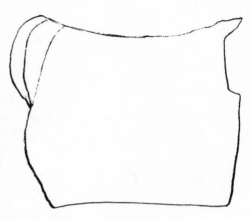

Peter (the boy on the left in the photograph) created the four drawings here. He was intent on solving the problem of rendering the "all purpose" art room pitcher. His classmate Benjy (on the right) had asked me to pose because he couldn't interest anyone else in standing still long enough.

In the second photograph Peter reflects on the drawing (shown above), while Benjy concentrates on his model to decide how to use his pencil to draw what he sees.

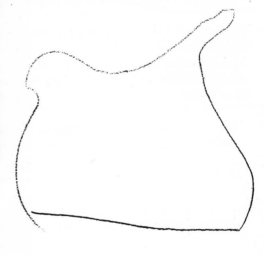

The pictures on these two pages show not only one child's use of a drawing technique, but also the quite different working methods of the two children shown. In teaching if we lead each child to develop his own interests and abilities he will regard art as more than just a required part of learning.

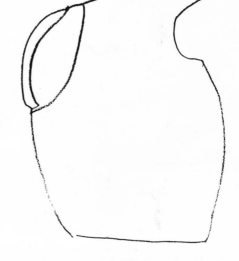

In the photograph above, Benjy holds up his drawing for my reaction. Peter looks up for a minute to see what his neighbor has accomplished, and then (in the photograph below) returns to his series of pitcher drawings while Benjy considers what he'll do next.

Buildings are an especially good subject for drawing. Their diverse shapes and sizes, the patterns created by doors and windows, lend themselves to interesting compositions, whether drawn as seen or as imagined. Here are two approaches to creating architecture compositions. In one, Dana, age seven, has selected the view from our art room window for his soft pencil drawing. St. Mark's Church, an imposing part of the view, has been a constant inspiration for children who cherish the discipline of trying to put down "exactly" what they see. Eric, also a seven-year-old, made a quick crayon drawing from imagination of what buildings at the New York World's Fair might be like. Later, his visits to the Fair made him feel he had really imagined the right colors and shapes.

Children enjoy making drawings of still life set-ups. The two sketches here by seven-year-olds show how they saw and drew the objects in their own individual ways. Peter looked at the forms in relation to each other and to the background. As he was working on his charcoal drawing (left) he explained, "I'm getting it down the way it looks — but quickly." Nancy showed the size relationships, moving away from the base line concept by placing the shapes in the same relative position in her cray-paz drawing that she had set for them on the table.

These four drawings were made by four very different children. During the second grade, wide differences in growth and development show up — as they did two years earlier and as they tend to once again in the very early period of adolescence. The seven- to eight-year-old is learning to further refine his motor control, to move outside himself, and to be more able and willing to see new symbols. He enjoys using the "tools" of art, and his expanding vision allows him to look for more than that which meets the eye.

"Still Life" drawings offer an ideal opportunity to take a long and careful look at relationships. Two or three children, working together, arrange their items — pots, vases, irons(an endless number of possibilities exists), and then select the angle from which they prefer to work. They then decide what kind of a still life drawing they want to make. Some choose to create a complex composition — a number of items placed beautifully on the paper; others prefer to concentrate on one item, investigating its form, texture, and color.

For a number of reasons still life is an ideal subject. Unlike a model, still life doesn't move or tire of posing. Then, too, if the model that children are drawing is a peer, there may be anxiety that the drawings won't be "good enough" and will offend the model. Still life presents no such problems. This helps some children to feel more at ease, and they feel free to devote themselves to experimenting — depicting the object as they see it, changing and re-arranging should the need arise.

Left: black paper with many different whites allowed Carolyn, age twelve, to capture the forms of three plant holders.

An old earthenware Mexican pot appears in drawings by eleven- and thirteen-year-olds. Richard, using the pot and a glass, worked with cray-paz and chalks to show the relationship of the two forms (below). Donald combined charcoal, pastels, and water colors (left) to create a brightly colored version of the pot and beautiful dried flowers.

Mixing media, Geof [right] and Danny created the compositions here that use pitcher and dried leaves as the central theme. They worked on manila paper and used watercolors, chalks, inks, and wash.

While Danny and Geof each achieved a very personal statement based on a similar still life, Noah selected the battered coffee pot and in his drawing gave it a completely new life.

Combining felt tipped markers and cray-paz, Barnaby (age six) transformed a piece of off-white muslin into this magnificent wall hanging.

So many things are possible rendering the simplest objects by means of the simplest techniques! The variations are endless. Children love to explore the world around them — discover what it really looks like as they observe, and what it may become as they draw. The most humble objects, such as the paintbrush container (shown on page six), classroom pitcher, or earthenware jug, are interesting to look at and to draw. Often a child will discover a "favorite" thing that he will render with special care or, perhaps, return to again and again. The favorite object shown here is a large green glass bottle. Carolyn used it in a composition on black paper; here, (top) it is part of another composition. Cathy, working with water color and chalk on wet paper, used both the bottle and a pot for her composition (below). The dried flowers, which were easily moved from pot to bottle, made it possible to try different combinations.

Eron, age seven, produced the still life on the left, using crayons and pastels. She placed the emphasis on the bottle and smaller pots. The flowers are of secondary importance, though still very much a part of the total composition.

Abbie, also a seven-year-old, drew a still life in which a delicately outlined bottle is central, and the flowers it holds are a most important part of her composition (right).

In attempting to help young children become aware of the relation of objects to each other in space we experimented by placing a number of objects in various positions on a work table. Some were lined up adjacent to each other; others were placed so that parts were hidden and the shapes looked different. Some children preferred the first arrangement; "Then we know that none of the parts are missing because we show them all!" Others thought it was "more interesting" and "it doesn't look like soldiers lined up" when the latter arrangement was discussed. "Also, lots of things are in front of each other when we happen to look at them, aren't they?" What evolved from this discussion was "It doesn't mean that parts are missing just because we don't show them!" For many, this realization opened up a whole new set of possibilities to explore in their drawing. After the discussion, the children working at each table set up a different still life arrangement. Then, after looking at it from all sides, each child decided where he wanted to sit to see it from the "best" view.

68

The green bottle with a sprig of eucalyptus was drawn by Posy using India ink on a wet white paper. The pitcher was filled with these sprigs and some ivy. A few bits of plant were placed on the table to complete this beautiful composition (right).

The incentive to move ahead, to discover new possibilities, takes different forms at different times. The experience described above is only one way to lead children to a new way of "seeing" and drawing. If good prints are available, we have used these, showing children that artists have their own style of drawing or painting a "still life."

Connie is shown diligently working with India ink, drawing the dried leaves and bottle. The finished drawing is at the right. A wash effect was introduced to allow the bottle to remain translucent. "Wash" is basically ink or tempera diluted so that it can be brushed or sponged onto the working surface.

69

Drawing means many different things to different people. That it is a vital part of an art curriculum and the ground work for using other art media is unquestioned. A painter or sculptor does quick sketches and makes many changes before he is ready to tackle his new work. A craftsman draws many versions of his pot, jewelry or textile design before he goes to work in the final medium. Certainly there are some very fine and capable artists who prefer working directly in the medium of their choice; but they continue to use drawings and quick sketches in the evolution of an idea until it seems "right" and ready for the canvas or the clay.

For children, drawing can mean learning to really look at an object to understand how it moves in space, how it relates to other objects around it. Drawing may try to capture "exactly" what the eye sees. Or it may allow imagination to soar by offering freedom to change the world — to use colors as they have never been used before, to create combinations of shapes, textures and lines that come from the inner self. This vision is one's own, quite unlike any other.

It is sometimes difficult to tell where drawing ends and painting begins. Young children often use paints as a drawing medium, using the brush in the same way they would use crayon or charcoal. Perhaps this is why a six-year-old said of painting, "It's a different kind of drawing — it's wet!" And a nine-year-old said, "Painting is drawing skill with liquid."

When we observe the work of artists we note that many combine drawing and painterly techniques at times. To understand the "idea" of painting technique, children need to be able to think about mass and form as compared with the line technique they so often use. There is no need to segregate these "ways of working." As they manipulate the tools of art, learn techniques, children see that there are possibilities for combining many media and styles. They become aware that there is more than one way to create a picture.

We tend to think of drawing as involving "dry" media, and painting as involving "wet" media, and much of the time this is true. Yet, media may be mixed and combined. Thus, it is not simply a matter of the work being clearly either a drawing or a painting. It may partake of the quality of each. Then, it is the emphasis placed upon line, produced by tools designed to produce line, or the emphasis on mass and value relationships achieved by media best suited to this approach, that determines whether a work is more clearly a drawing or a painting. Examples of mixed media work have been seen on previous pages, and others will be found on pages to follow.

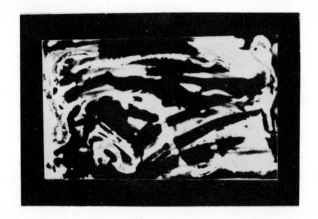

Mixing media adds a new dimension to drawing or painting experiences. At times it is just not possible to achieve a certain special effect with just one medium; feeling free to use anything that will help to solve such a problem opens up a new way of thinking about materials and enhances a child's work.

Painting and drawing usually involve a wide variety of colors, and children are asked to make many choices and decisions regarding the right combination for a particular work. Colors are used beautifully much of the time, but often taken for granted — used, but their magnificence is not necessarily perceived. To instill a conscious sensitivity to this beauty is not easy. One could talk about it — and get nowhere. Or one might try to isolate certain combinations and seek to help children heighten their awareness of these colors. This is an instance of a prescribed limitation (in this case, the number of colors to be used) that is constructive, as it leads to a keener appreciation and more effective use of color in general.

What happens when children are "limited" to working with black and white? Most of the time we use manila paper; for this session we used black construction paper. White chalk, white crayons, white pastels, white cray-paz, and white inks were set out. White paper with a similar variety of black media was also made available. It was suggested that they try not only the white media on black paper, and *vice versa,* but also the black paper with the black media, and white with the white.

At first, the reactions were a mixture of disbelief and amusement. A seven-year-old summed up the feelings of everyone with "Can't we use even *one* color? How can we do anything with just black and white? It's impossible! It won't work — black on black — that's funny!" For six- and seven-year-olds this was an unbelievable experience. Expecting to have nothing show on the black paper they were astounded at the number of "blacks" they achieved, depending upon how hard they pressed, or the kind of medium they used.

Turning to white on black and the reverse, they found it possible to create textures they had not achieved with previous drawings and paintings. When they started work they chose small pieces of paper, not sure that they would want to do very much; soon they requested larger and larger paper as their caution changed to the pleasure of experimenting — even though they were not working with color.

Eight-year-olds scoffed. "It just won't show. Let's do something else." I took up a black crayon and drew a simple shape on my black paper. It did show! "Try the cray-paz!" "And the charcoal!" As I continued to demonstrate they tried to guess how each different black medium would look. When I brushed a black paint wash over the black crayon (heavily used, originally,), the result was a joy! Since wax and water don't mix, the wash left a bubble-like effect wherever the crayon had not been applied. The variation of blacks was intriguing to them, and now no one doubted that it worked; each chose a piece of paper and started exploring the possibilities.

In the photographs above, twelve-year-olds are using white media on black paper. Eli (left) draws a plant in an earthenware pot. Carolyn (on the right) completes her work (illustrated on page 64) with a few last strokes of chalk. A classmate is working from the same still life seen from a different point of view. Below is shown a complete work, with a wallpaper design included to enhance the composition.

Eighth-graders depict dream-like experiences, using both wet and dry media. Jenny imagined herself alone in a forest (above). Angela also used a forest as her subject, but in her picture a large animal ambles among the trees (right).

In these two pictures, the children achieved a painterly effect. Black ink was used for mass as well as line work; chalk or opaque paint was available for changing forms which required working over. With white media on black paper, areas of grey were created. The more the pictures were worked on, the more beautiful certain areas became. Black ink created unusual darks and lights, depending upon the degree of dilution. The overall effect was of dramatic contrasts of white and black, and areas where there were subtle gradations, and unusual textures.

A variety of textures was created by combining media. Some of the possibilities are as follows: chalk rubbed gently over the black paper which was first placed on a textured surface; a semi-wet brush lightly carried over a dry surface; black wash over white pastel, chalk, or crayon; removing sections of a medium by using the handle of the brush to draw into the surface. As different needs arose, the children found a way to solve each problem, until the work was considered complete and ready for evaluation.

Further experimentation might involve the use of any two colors, or whatever similar limitation seems valid. The aim is to help children become aware of the range of possibilities within what initially seemed to be deprivation! Further, we are so accustomed to having too many choices, many children welcome an occasional limitation with great relief.

Emily, a seventh-grader, prepared her palette and now sets to work.

"ART EXPRESSES WHAT YOU THINK ABOUT THINGS, WHAT
THEY TELL YOU, AND WHAT THEY LOOK LIKE TO YOU."
— EIGHT-YEAR-OLD

5 COLOR AND PAINT

Stop what you are doing for one minute and take a long and careful look around. Are you really "seeing" your surroundings? Seeing them in their full color? Or is everything in shades of grey?

In order to cope with all of the bustling activities around us we learn to block out extraneous matters, leaving ourselves free to devote attention to the "essentials" of existence. Sometimes this results in blocking out colors as well! Now take another look. Has the veil lifted? Even the dreariest area has some color. Take a close look at a brick wall and observe the variations in color and texture. Depending upon the direction of the light source — whether it be the sun, a candle, or electric bulb — lights and darks vary. The same beauty and variety of colors may be seen everywhere — in people moving about, fruit placed in a bowl, clothes hanging on a line, cans on the grocery shelf. Everyday experiences which we take for granted might offer delight if we but *looked* at them instead of relegating them to a world of greys.

What a delight it is to observe the subtle and almost infinite range of colors so generally taken for granted. This variety is the result of combinations of the primary colors. Children first become consciously aware of color when they are given the opportunity to mix red, yellow, and blue in as many different ways as they can find. Often such early mixing experiences result in something that is rather mud-like.

When given pure intense colors it's such fun to put drops of many colors in a jar lid and see the marble-like effect as the colors form ribbons around each other. If small amounts of paint are used, there is no need to be concerned about waste. Having had such "mixing" experiences, children will be better able to experiment and feel free to use a wide range of colors as they paint or draw. Even more importantly, they will have become aware of the beauty of color and a whole new world will have opened up.

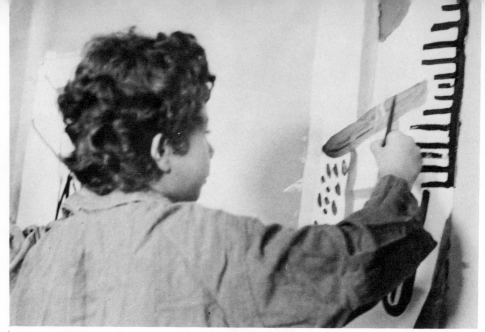

Pam, age nine, works on a design. Soon after starting she realized the paper was not large enough; we taped an extra piece to the first and she was able to continue.

Middle- and upper-graders learn to set the mood or tone of a painting from color mixing experiments. They are amazed at the number of variations possible even when limited to two colors, such as red and blue (the kind of limitation discussed in the previous section). With black and white also available, a drop or two of either will create unexpected changes.

Color mixed for a painting that there is not time to finish can be saved by covering the jar lid in which it was mixed with plastic or foil; a bit of water will rejuvenate the paint even a week later. Saving specially mixed colors becomes really important, and a shelf set aside for such items assures the students that their paints will be available when next they have the opportunity to work.

Emily, twelve, takes a long look at her painting. The sketch (above the painting) was made quickly on a trip and she had to reconstruct the scene, combining what she remembered with what was noted on the sketch.

Painting is a two-fold delight. There is the satisfaction of being engrossed in a project, and the satisfaction of a job well done. In the picture above, Beth, a thirteen-year-old, uses water color and tempera for her still life. Below, she poses happily with her finished painting.

79

Children will have their own ideas to share as they "discover" new color combinations, and they will be filled with delight at the seemingly endless possibilities.

When setting up a room for painting, there may be need for flexibility regarding this medium as with many others presented. One or two children in the group may have had terrible painting experiences in the past and may, as a result, refuse to paint. This refusal needs to be accepted temporarily. Thirty other children are waiting for the word "GO!" Special jobs or other activities should be found for the children that are unwilling to paint so that the teacher is able to function effectively with the rest of the class. Then, it is important to try to find out how to help each individual child who is intimidated by the painting assignment to overcome his concern.

I have never found that forcing a child to do something was good for him, for the others in the class, or for the teacher. Peers often side with the child; the teacher only jeopardizes her position in the eyes of the children by undue pressuring, and nothing is solved. Unless insistence is the method suggested by a school psychologist because a certain child needs such unusual treatment, it should not be used.

The teacher will find that at another time it may be possible to discover the child's reasons for not wanting to work with certain media, and work with him toward a solution. We might also consider whether everyone should always be expected to use the same medium at the same time. An art program should not be "either/or." At times one medium is offered, at other times a range of choices ought to be available.

Evaluating art is no less difficult for the child than it is for the adult. Setting a standard for "what is good" remains a problem, because it has so many dimensions. Here Paul and Alan look at each other's paintings. They cannot help but be concerned with "How does mine look compared with his?" or "I wonder how he thinks mine looks?" While we attempt to avoid a competitive atmosphere, we find that children are always judging themselves in terms of their peers. If we help them to learn how to handle self and peer evaluation, competition will not become an unhealthy and negative demon.

Young children are less concerned about evaluation than are the older children of middle and upper grades. Yet even they need to have many opportunities to hear constructive comment on their work. The teacher's way of handling critical evaluation, when needed, becomes the model. When children begin to make their own comparisons and evaluative remarks, the pattern set by the teacher should help them relate to their peers positively, using their own language and means of expressing their criticism — whether positive or negative. This spirit of understanding and constructive attitude is not a mere mimicry of words they have heard the teacher speak; it is a reflection of an inner attitude of acceptance which each of them (hopefully) has experienced himself and seen is given to others equally consistently.

Creating the proper and constructive atmosphere for criticism is so very important. Saying "That stinks . . . look at how great mine is!" may offer momentary pleasure for a child for some reason, but the fellow thus insulted can be counted on for a return bout. Yet we cannot be "iron fisted" in our insistence on a totally "charitable" exchange during evaluation sessions — or at any other time, for that matter. There are moments when we should guide, and moments when we should overlook what is said. The important thing is knowing the difference. No doubt, children will occasionally torment each other with insults and other means; we cannot expect to be present at every turn and hear every remark. It would be terribly unfair if we were. Learning to cope with such problems for himself is part of each child's "growing pains." We *do* care about each one, we attempt to help each one learn to evaluate and to learn from his peers, his teachers and through his own honest self-evaluation. But we must realize what is serious and what not. Some of the things children say to each other are quite funny, they cannot

Listening to music as he painted, Michael, a six-year-old, moved his feet up and down and applied his brush with lines and dots to the same rhythm. A loud "BOOM" led him to fill in the section of the paper on the lower left quickly.

help laughing themselves. Unless there is real hostility involved, they tend to mimic adult actions they have observed and been subjected to themselves. We, as adults, have quite a bit to learn from such experiences as well!

Children sometimes "check" each other, turning what might have become an explosive situation into an opportunity to care even more about exchanging "ideas" about their work. Sometimes they share colors, but one color may not look quite the same on one painting as it does on another. Then they begin to wonder and to ask "Why?" What colors are touching? Are these different? Was one applied thick, the other watered down? Is the quality of paper the same? Were the brushes first used with a different color and did this change the new one? So many questions come to mind as possibilities — and the children will ask even more.

There are times when combining art experiences helps a child who is somewhat worried about his own work. For example, listening to music that was being played during one art session, Michael seemed to forget that only minutes before he had said he wouldn't paint today because someone had smeared his work. Furious, he could only think in terms of doing the same to the other fellow's painting. At such a time, theory makes no sense, and saying "two wrongs don't make a right" may simply not work. I quickly moved him to another place and gave him fresh paints and brushes. He worked, but he couldn't really forget that his other painting had been ruined. He might not have really liked it particularly, but seeing it spoiled suddenly gave it great significance. The memory of that last experience clouded his enthusiasm about painting this time. But the music was enticing; he couldn't keep himself from painting even though he tried.

Music may be a planned and at the same time a "casual" part of any art session. Whether used or not depends upon many things: the availability of equipment, the nature of the art assignment, the needs of particular children. The use of music — and the music used — should be completely flexible. I don't believe it is necessary to have a list of records suitable for particular circumstances. If a range is available — classical, folk, popular, and children's — the teacher may select whatever will best suit the specific need. It is possible to use music to help children solve a given problem, or to be an inspiration for compositions, as in the example above, in which the "movements" of the music became the subject of Michael's work. On occasion it may be provided for the pure pleasure of simply listening and relaxing.

Children depict themselves and their experiences in many ways.

One may be a strong man in a circus, another is an elegant lady with yellow hair (above). In the picture below the child shows himself as part of a team. As the batter he warms up to do his best when he is at bat.

In their art children find fresh ways to depict space and time. In the work above a child shows his classmates touring the Statue of Liberty. They are actually climbing the stairs inside, but depicted this way the form of the statue is clear at the same time. In another drawing (center right) a child shows the positions of four couples in a square dance set. The ten seconds of a countdown are illustrated in the painting at the right.

Two of the aspects of a city were chosen as subjects by the children whose paintings are shown here. One captures the violence of demolition that clears away old buildings to make way for new construction. The other depicts the symmetry and anonymity of buildings on one of the city's streets.

When buildings are the subject for drawing or painting, each child may use his own daily experiences to advantage. Whether in the city or the suburbs, buildings vary in size and shape. They serve specific functions — living, offices, manufacturing, storage — and each takes on a style of its own. As we move about our daily business, we tend to see such buildings in groups rather than as individual forms.

In assigning buildings as a subject, it helps to suggest to the children that they slow down, stop awhile — and look at individual buildings. There is so much to discover! What are they used for? What were the building materials? If there is an old building, what might it have been like originally? It is good to do a quick sketch if possible. Then, one begins to see a building or group of buildings with a new eye.

The kinds of questions one asks the children, or the children ask themselves, will vary depending upon the aims of the assignment. In the one for which the paintings opposite were done, we wanted to focus on the essence of the experience — the feeling of the city each child had as he explored the area of his choice. The result of moodiness, coolness, or heated activity came through as children moved from the visual experience to a verbal discussion and then to a visual statement with paint.

Awareness is the key. Once children are helped to become aware and sensitive to their surroundings, they are ready to differentiate whether form is used beautifully or awkwardly to suit the function. They begin to learn to evaluate, an important step in the development of critical thinking. It is so easy to always be against things, but to be able to understand and say "why," and to make constructive suggestions for improvement — this is another story.

The work shown is by nine-year-olds, but such experiences can be offered to children at different age levels. For six-year-olds, a walk around the block, looking and talking about the different buildings, will help them to know their immediate surroundings at school. When older children take trips with a school bus, they pass through different parts of town. Alerting them to the remarkable variety of buildings, the many diverse and interesting styles, helps them to see what might otherwise be   disregarded or seen only as a blur. For all children, such experiences are important, and many more opportunities to take a close look at other daily experiences often taken for granted should be suggested.

Bored with the number of windows needed to depict the Empire State Building, this fourth-grader asked whether he had to include them all. Reassured that this was not necessary, he completed his drawing by adding "etc., etc., etc."

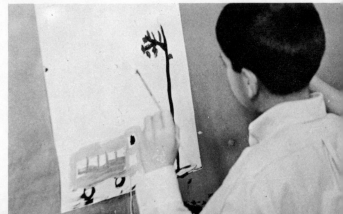

Right: Jon, age six, worked in large areas of color, adding a few pieces of bright colored tissue papers and some roping to complete the painting. A discussion of texture preceded this work time. A few different textures were placed on the table near the painting supplies. Children were free to use them if they felt their painting could use more texture than it was possible to achieve with paint alone.

Bottom: Dana, age eight, decided he didn't like his painting; it came out very different from his original idea. He quickly brushed over parts of it, achieving a muddy effect through which some of the autumn colors seemed to stand out. Suddenly interested again, he turned his brush around. Using the back end he drew into the wet paint. He was amazed with the result since the tool removed some of the paint and the color of the paper came through wherever he had drawn.

Painting assignments should be varied so that the children will realize the full potential of the paint medium. This means exploring the many possible ways to use paint, not just the many different subjects that may be painted. Occasionally, art sessions may be devoted to experimenting. For example, the teacher suggests trying such techniques as applying paint with semi-dry brush, painting on wet paper, or incising lines in thickly applied paint. The possibilities of achieving textures with paint alone and then also by adding other materials to the painted surface may be pointed out. This latter technique is an introduction to collage as well as an approach to the subject of texture itself.

This, and the painting on the next page, were the result of color mixing experiences after seeing an excellent film. The problem presented to the children was to see how many variations and combinations they could discover when mixing red, yellow, and blue — the primary colors.

Some of the questions I asked the children were in relation to what they had seen in the film (*Discovering Color*, Film Associates of California). Now they had the opportunity to experiment themselves. What we wanted to check on was:

Do you really find orange if you mix a little red and a little yellow? What happens when you use more red than yellow? — or more yellow than red? How much red and how much blue do you need to make purple? — and what happens when blue and yellow are mixed?

Adam covered his entire paper with a design.

Further experiments were based on such questions as: How do the colors change when a bit of white or black is added? What happens when you paint these colors next to each other? — or on a piece of colored paper? The children had had many opportunities to mix colors previously; this was an attempt to help them become aware that they could mix a specific color, rather than depending upon finding it accidently.

Noah, age ten, was devoted to this painting. He described exactly how he conceived it — a design growing and looking like a pinwheel in motion. He returned to work on it whenever possible. In the morning he would rush into the art room for just a second to check on how a special color had dried, and ask me if I would let him come in sometime during the day to work on it. Then he would clear the special work time with his classroom teacher. While this was not always possible, we tried our best to give him ample opportunity to complete the painting — a gift for his father.

"Trees, flowers and a little bug playing in the grass" is the way a six-year-old described his painting.

Inspiration for painting varies. Sometimes a trip experience helps children discover something that is "perfect" for a painting; for others, the opportunity to use brush and paint is inspiration enough. Sometimes they will prefer to paint subjects; at other times they will be more satisfied creating beautiful, abstract patterns. They might depict thoughts concerning outer space and the launching pad — placing themselves in the "driver's" seat; they might create quickly executed or carefully planned "designs." The teacher who has had the experience of painting recently will certainly be better prepared to respond to the problems as well as the pleasures the children encounter in their search for the subject matter and painting method that will be the most satisfying.

"When I walk to school this is what I see." Steven shows workmen on the left digging up the road. Between two red lights are three children on their way to school; to the right is a policeman. Behind them all, the traffic moves swiftly by.

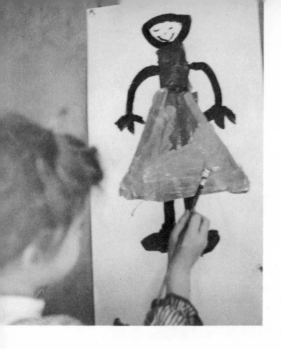

Here are two children's use of the figure as a subject for their paintings. Laura, a seven-year-old, painted a picture of a lady. She began by "drawing" the body. Then, she added the dress (shown in the photograph). Eventually, she put on the hair, and the painting (lower left) was finished. Paul, age eight, chose to paint the Statue of Liberty (lower right). He depicted her as a powerful figure looking very much like the Indians he was learning about at the time. Reproduced in color on page 83 is another eight-year-old's version of the famous statue.

In their desire to depict experiences realistically Connie, age twelve, and Kara, thirteen, combine drawing and painting techniques. They found that by blocking in the forms with a light-colored wash, it was possible to plan ahead without being limited by the original light wash drawing. Too often, when a pencil is used for the initial sketch, the result is a rigid painting. By planning with paint one does not become so involved with the details as to find it impossible to change or rearrange forms as desired.

The art period is a very special time for children. It is most successful if the teacher has carefully planned how the session is to proceed. On these two pages is a description of how one painting class was handled; the photographs record the progress of two of the children in the class.

We spent about five minutes discussing how to handle the paints, mixing cups and water, and assigned two children to be on clean-up duties. Young children vie for this opportunity so we keep a check list to be sure no one misses out on the pleasure and privilege of clean-up work.

Children moved from the discussion area to the easels and painting tables in groups of twos and threes to avoid a traffic jam. Some preferred to work on the tables, as they had not yet learned to control the dripping that the upright position of the easel at first incurs. They passed the tray with brushes. They knew they could choose three different sizes. Paints were already set out at the work places, as were water containers for brush-washing. Those who felt they were ready to move to the work area went first. I was then able to have quiet talks with anyone who thought he had a problem or who needed attention before getting to work. Painting paper was tacked to the easels or set out on the tables. Each child could choose to work at the spot where a paper that was "just right" for his painting idea would be available. Those who came over last could request a different paper if they did not find the size they needed.

Eric and David spent about fifteen minutes working on their first paintings. Since there was still time available, they could easily start and complete the second paintings as well. Sometimes, if there are only five or ten minutes left at the end of a class it is a good idea to suggest that those who have finished a painting move to a table where drawing supplies are available. It seems much easier to do a "short" drawing with so little time left; this makes good use of the time. A child without something to do who is allowed to drift around the room tends to disturb those still at work.

Eric and David, first-graders, paint at the same easel, each absorbed in his own work. Eric contemplates what to do next (left) and then completes the features with a quick brush stroke for the nose (right).

Eric puts the brush into another color (left) and stretches himself up to his tip-toes to reach the spot where he can paint in the hair (right). He holds his brush with both hands, using a circular motion to apply the paint. He is making unusual sounds "like happy groaning," according to David, who suddenly looks up from his own work to see what is happening.

Stepping back for a second, David went to work again (left). Eric finished his painting with a brilliant sun. "Mrs. Greenberg, I'm ready for another painting paper!" With the same color used for the hair Eric had quickly painted in a mustache. On the right is the completed painting.

David was soon finished with his painting too. Another paper was put up for each of the boys, and they immediately became engrossed in their second pictures.

93

"Wondering" is so much a part of growing up. "I wonder how . . ." or, "I wonder if . . ." or, "I wonder why . . ." are so often heard as children discuss their real or hoped-for experiences, their fantasies and their dreams. Art can lead children to express some of the things they wonder about, or lead them to speculate about new things. This happened when Andy, a fifth grader, did a painting of a man.

What happens to trees as the seasons change? Do they turn upside down? What would the world look like if everything had different colors?

For most of his painting Andy used a fine pointed brush, drawing with the point. His first step was to use a wash — some thinned out paint — to block in the form. Then he went over this light color with the colors he wanted to use to show the miner. "No, it's not me," he said, in response to someone's question. "But it sure looks like you!" "Well, maybe. But this is a miner — see the coal on his face? And he's smoking a big cigar. I can smell it! I wonder how I'll look when I'm old?"

What does a person look like? Or what would a person look like if you made him up from your world of wondering. If he's moving here and there, maybe he needs more legs to move faster. The picture at the left was done by Marc, age seven. He shows a lady moving her hands around as she talks.

As a child experiments with showing his world of fantasy and wonderment he is also becoming more aware of — and sensitive to — his own surroundings. Given opportunities to bring out *his ideas* (far more meaningful to him than those we might have suggested), he learns to expand and to manipulate his visual, tactile and aural senses.   As he learns to stretch his imagination, he finds pleasure and gains confidence in his ability to solve his own problems, leaning less and less on the adults around him.

He experiments to see what happens when paint is applied heavily, when it is thinned out and translucent, when it is applied to wet paper, and dry, the effect of thick and thin lines, mass in relation to line, dark values contrasted to light. These early experiments lead toward technical understanding, and children are then able to solve drawing or painting problems, achieving their own desired result. Experimentation continues, and new ways of working evolve, but these later experiences have a foundation in the technical awareness that was built through the early years of learning and working.

The teacher is always at hand, ready to guide the children as needed. She makes remarks to one or another that will help them find the right path, sensitive to what is vital at that moment. She is appreciative of success, and honest in her evaluation when the children know that they themselves could have done a better job.

This is part of a project on which many children worked together. The photograph shows a detail of a 5′ x 12′ mural. Before beginning the painting, the fifth grade children had taken a trip to a Mennonite farm. They had studied life on the farm for three days and made many sketches. When they returned from the trip, they began work. First, they sorted out the many "topics" their sketches represented, and listed them in order of importance. Then they planned the mural itself and where the various things they had sketched and observed would appear. Each child requested to work on the section that most interested him, or for which he had made a good quick sketch that was needed. Sometimes, in a project such as this, at the point children select the area on which they want to work, it seems that everyone selects the same two or three areas. When that happens, a revision of the original plan is in order. The "unattractive" areas may not have been as important to the overall work as originally assumed.

Correlation of art with the activities of other classes has an important place in the curriculum. A drawing or a painting may be a natural followup to an important class experience. Art has great value when used to augment and consolidate history, social studies or science projects. It should never be used exclusively in this manner though; there should also be time allowed for art as a pure art experience. This is to say art has its own integral value, as well as being a useful "tool." The truly balanced and exciting curriculum is the one in which art and classroom teachers work together, sometimes tying the art experiences (whether in the classroom or art studio) to contemporary or historic events, and at other times allowing the children to explore the limitless expressive possibilities of art as a marvellous adventure in itself.

One way in which correlation may be achieved with success is mural painting. Whether it is the result of a class trip or of social studies involving some special experiences that might be enhanced by a large painting, the mural may be used to bring together into a unified whole what has been learned. Also, the mural is one of the projects in which many children can be involved at one time.

Third-graders sponge sky and grass colors onto a large sheet of Kraft (brown wrapping) paper. As they work, others discuss what they think ought to be painted onto the surface, and where. When a class is large, it is often easier to list the different ideas and eliminate those that seem less important. Then, some children can paint right on the background, while others draw or paint sections at their desks or tables. These are later cut by the child, and placed on the mural as originally planned. Thus, everyone will be able to work on some of the mural.

If at all possible, groups of five or six working at one mural will gain much more from the experience than an entire class vying for a place to work. Perhaps if a number of different murals are needed during a school semester, every child can have the opportunity to be part of a small group once or twice. Otherwise this becomes a fragmented experience with no real meaning to the individual.

A mural offers a special opportunity for the classroom teacher and the art teacher to work together. They will gain a deeper understanding and appreciation of the resource materials each is able to bring to the class. This cooperation or "partnership" in teaching will inspire the pupils not only to seek additional information, but also to emulate the spirit of "working together." There are too few opportunities for such experiences.

Emily and Geof discuss their section of the eighth-grade mural, trying to reach agreement about the placement of different pictorial elements. The mural paper is behind them, tacked to a large class room bulletin board.

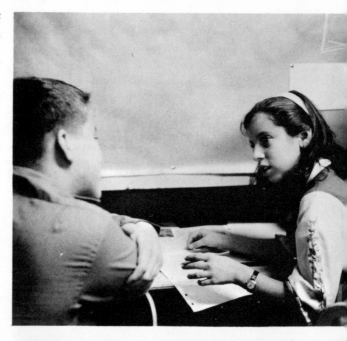

A group of eighth-graders are sketching in chalk to plan their mural. For reference material they are using sketches and photographs taken by classmates, as well as memories of the recent trip experience. Above the paper on which they are sketching is a mural completed the previous year by another group. The new mural will replace it. Since the mural and the paint supplies are at the back of this classroom, each child is able to do some work when he has free time. Committees for different sections of the mural keep each other informed of progress, and at times, work started by one child will be completed by his committeemate. Since this is a group project and each committee has set similar standards of what is to be achieved, such sharing of the work is possible. In setting up committees, the teacher needs to keep in mind not only what the children are especially interested in, but also whether the members of a particular group will be able to work together. Two children constantly at odds will not help the committee to function. On the other hand, it is quite possible that these children will overcome their dislike for each other, and a new and pleasant relationship will evolve.

A somewhat different form of "mural" is the stage backdrop — a freely worked and somewhat exaggerated painting that helps to create a mood or a specific idea meant to enhance a play or other stage presentation. Here, areas need to be large; few details are required, since these tend to be lost when seen from the back of a school auditorium. Children in the audience as well as those on stage learn that simplicity is the key. When too much "happens" in the backdrop, then the action on stage, the spoken lines, and the costumes are all "fighting" each other.

Correlation of subject matter involving other areas of the curriculum with the use of art materials can aid in cooperative working experiences. There may be a definite event to be depicted (such as George Washington crossing the Delaware). Since we do not have a photographic record of such historic subjects, there is wide latitude in how the children may depict them. It is not necessary to assume that the artists of recent years had the only "right" idea of what the pictorial images were. Children should be allowed to depict their own version of an historic situation. They are able to gather many facts through reading and classroom discussions and should do so before starting the art work involved. But they should not be asked to copy or trace some artist's or illustrator's interpretation. An exercise in copying has no connection with art as we are discussing it here. It is time-consuming and can be considered nothing more than busy work. To gather facts from many sources, and, based on this information, to attempt to re-create and depict an historical event, can become an experience long remembered.

Other opportunities for correlating learning experiences are shown on this page. The banners and cloth hangings of the Middle Ages were inspiration for the two cloth banners shown above. Laura, whose work appears on the left, and Ann, whose work is shown on the right, combined tempera, watercolor, cray-paz, and felt markers to create these designs on sheeting. With dowels attached, top and bottom, they were easily hung for display. When worked on both sides, such banners are very beautiful.

Fresco, using either the wet or dry method, is a painting technique the children in the fifth grade learned about from visiting The Cloisters and The Metropolitan Museum. Here, Ann used water colors on a background made from plaster-coated masonite. Heavy cardboard may also be used. The surface is easily worked on while still wet; as it dries it can either be sponged wet again, or worked on dry for finishing details.

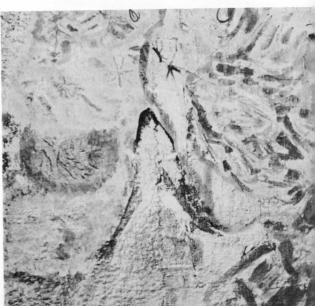

Art constantly offers new challenges for discovery and opportunities for self-expression. It is like the proverbial well that never runs dry — the cruet that never empties. If art is presented to children in these terms, if the children are led to see its potential and feel increasing satisfaction with their own art experiences, they will never bog down or find it a bore. Having worked for years in an atmosphere in which they experimented with many media and explored ever new ways of creating images and designs, children considered by many to be in the "declining" period of creativity continue to bloom. They have individual interests, and as seen in the work on this page by twelve- and thirteen-year-olds, they treasure the opportunity to share them with others through drawing and painting.

For her picture (upper left), Connie worked with cray-paz on sandpaper to achieve an unusual effect. The "toothiness" of sand paper offered a new experience which many children found enticing. George used water colors for his still life (above right). He combined chalk with the paints for part of the design on the pitcher. Linda, in her abstract painting (below left) wanted to create forms blending into each other, and to emphasize mass rather than lines. At lower right is Ann's unfinished painting of a house in the country.

Ten-year-olds sketching at The Cloisters in New York City.

"ART IS SOMETHING BEAUTIFUL."
— EIGHT-YEAR-OLD

TAKING TRIPS

"Listen lady, are these kids with you? Well, you gotta get 'em up off the floor. We can't have kids sprawled on the floor in a museum. This looks like the beach! And those pencils! Suppose they mark up the walls? Or the art work? What if some adults came along now and saw you?"

Once, groups of children touring a museum were viewed with decided alarm. The attitude of museum guards, and of personnel in general, has changed within recent years — at least compared with our first experiences in taking children on trips that offered real opportunities for looking and learning. Junior Museums as well as excellent Museum Departments of Education offer guided tours with trained leaders who know something about children's growth and development as well as about art history. It is possible to make of every trip a rewarding and satisfying experience for everyone. Doing so requires much thoughtful planning to make the best possible use of the time allowed and the facilities available. It also requires that the teacher know how to allow children the maximum freedom — at the same time setting realistic limitations. There is no doubt that certain rules must be set and clearly understood before taking any trip. This framework of discipline helps children understand the limitations set, and the breadth of freedom which is theirs becomes important in making the trip a valid educational experience. A successful museum tour is not one in which children hurriedly march two-by-two through exhibition halls. This is too much restraint, and soon, unable to take a lingering look at whatever particularly interests them, the children will become bored and probably start poking each other. Children that are allowed to discover what interests them most in the experience will get much more out of it. It is true that even after years of exposure to the acceptable limitations of freedom there will always be someone who needs to poke and push. However, based on years of experience, I have found that the ratio of poor behavior is lowered as children learn how to use freedom. And as poor behavior decreases, learning, due to greater involvement, increases.

Unless there is a real reason and the children are well aware of what it is, a trip can be a meaningless experience and   a day away from so-called "work" rather than a chance to do and learn something special. While it is clearly the place to be visited that should be the major focus of attention, there are peripheral facits that enhance and broaden experience. Most often some form of transportation is required: school or public buses, private cars, subways. If the destination is a museum, where is it located on a city map? What are the possible routes — and which will we take? What direction will we travel from our school? How long will the ride take? When will we eat lunch? What exhibits will we see, and for how long? Can we buy souvenirs? When? How much money will we need? Even though some questions will seem unimportant, children who have an idea of the plan for the trip seem to be better able to sustain themselves than those who receive no information and constantly need to be reassured that there will be ample time for everything.

At the museum there are certain special exhibits to be seen; in some cases a movie may be shown, and a guide may be available (especially if plans are made well in advance) to answer questions as the tour progresses. Children who have some background in the subject matter of the trip, some understanding of the history and geography of the peoples whose work is being discussed, can ask intelligent questions, and are keenly interested in hearing good answers. With no previous preparation, children tend to lose interest, have private conversations, and wander off. Maximum background information and participation in planning insures maximum involvement and learning during the trip itself.

Middle- and upper-graders bring pencils and pads; they can be given sketching assignments and important questions to answer to offer a specific focus for the experience. The trip becomes somewhat of a "hunt" and involves most children more than they might otherwise be. They need to go beyond looking without really seeing, and this calls for concentration. A follow-up assignment might involve discussions of their reactions to what was seen, which will bring out new insights into the people and their way of life as studied through the works of art. This helps children learn that a trip is another way of learning. While it also involves a certain amount of "fun," it requires thinking, observing, and responding. They learn about museums (galleries, factories), and this introduction leads many to return on their own time to visit other displays and explore these vast rooms for new experiences.

The atmosphere at The Cloisters almost requires whispering even when one has something important to share. Here, Bill, off in one section of a large room, can sketch alone, surrounded by the beautiful works of art.

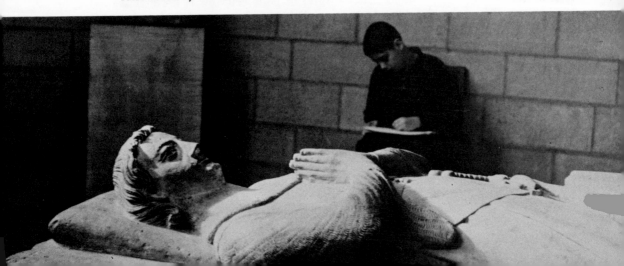

EEN HATSHEPSUT
1490 1480 B.C.   XVIII DYNASTY

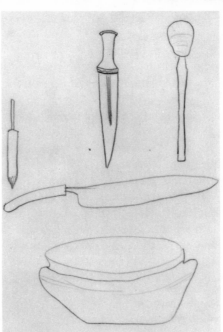

Sketches made by eleven-year-olds during a trip to the Egyptian rooms at The Metropolitan Museum of Art in New York City.

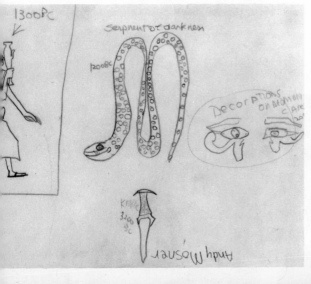

105

The guide helps to set the tone for the trip. If she knows that the members of your class have had some preparation in advance, she will adjust the tour to fit their understanding and their needs. She will know what is important to highlight, thereby adding to the children's store of knowledge. She keeps a steady pace because there is a schedule to follow, but remains flexible in how time is used, guided by the kind and amount of questions children ask at each point. After the "official" tour it is often possible for the children to return to certain exhibits where they can sketch or look for answers to specific questions asked in the specially prepared assignment sheet.

Eleven-year-olds moving about after a lecture, sketch or read points of information on labels which might otherwise be over-looked. Here (above) they are in the exhibition room of Indian sculpture in New York's Metropolitan Museum.

In the same museum, ten-year-olds take a second look at suits of armor after their guided tour (right).

106

During the trip, this time to The Metropolitan Museum's exhibit of Greek pottery, the children moved about in groups of three or four with sketch pads and question sheets in hand. For such trips, two, or even three adults should assist the teacher. Museums understandably do not like to have a group of children in a room unattended. With the teacher and two other adults, the children were able to work in three different adjacent rooms. The noise level is lower when such an arrangement is possible, and other museum visitors are not distracted from their viewing by swarms of children.

In the photograph above Peter shows the student teacher his sketch. Arnold looks up in awe as he sketches a large pot from the Red Attic period, and a group of girls look at Jane's work, momentarily distracted from their own sketches. They are sitting on rubber mats provided for such use by the museum. In the picture (above right), three of the boys are seen sketching and writing. The girls are involved again (right), each concentrating on reading the questions before moving to look at display cases in different parts of the room.

Susan

Trips like the one described on the previous page are experiences children will never forget. The impressions they record convey that it was all very worthwhile. In reacting to the trip, one boy wrote: "On a day when the autumn leaves were falling softly our class took a trip to The Metropolitan Museum of Art. Oh, how much fun it was when the guide took us on our tour. She showed us all kinds of pots from the ancient Greeks."

"However, I did not understand why the Greeks had to have a pot for every purpose. My mother has a pot that she uses for two, three, or four purposes. Sometimes I think the Greeks wanted to show off, but at other times I think that they thought if they had a pot for each purpose it would make cleaning easier." And a girl, new to the school, wrote: "I thought it was a special trip because when I used to go with my other school I used to say, 'Come on, let's go home.' But this time I'll say, 'Let's stay longer.'"

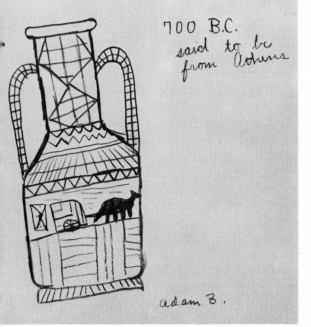

700 B.C.
said to be
from Athens

adam B.

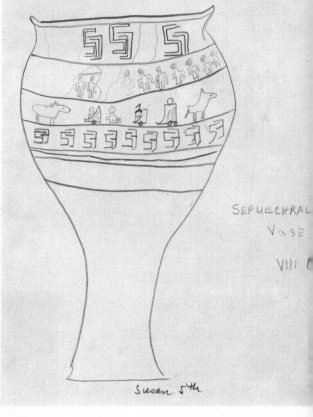

SEPULCHRAL
Vase
VIII C

Susan 5th

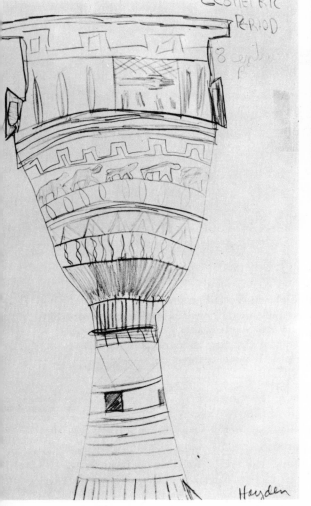

GEOMETRIC
PERIOD
8 century

Hayden

On these two pages are sketches made by the ten-year-olds who took the trip to the exhibit of Greek sculpture and pottery at The Metropolitan Museum.

Every part of a class excursion may be rewarding if properly planned. Even taking a school bus can be an exciting experience. Here, eight-year-olds are shown in the photograph as they were being led onto the school bus by their teacher. Each carried a shopping bag with lunch, as well as sketching pad and a soft lead pencil. They went to a farm in upstate New York for the day, which required a long ride in the bus. The teacher was prepared with songs and a guitar to help everyone relax during the trip. The children had books to read and some games to play. But they were also involved with observing the passing scene, seeing how it changed from the hustle and bustle of the city to the suburbs and then to the farmlands. When they arrived at their destination, in addition to collecting weeds, branches, walnuts, they toured the farm to see the work involved, to learn about the changes through the years. They enjoyed picnic lunches, sitting on the ground and taking pleasure in the crunchy sound of last year's leaves. As part of the plan for the day, the children occasionally sketched as they drove quickly past scenery along the highway as well as drawing the trees and buildings at the farm.

Lisa's sketch (left) of the tall grasses; as her drawing shows she looked carefully as they walked into these grasses and other sections of the woods near the farm house. Below is Steven's drawing of the farm and the surrounding country side — complete with compass directions.

Trip-taking may involve almost anything the children do as a group outside of their school — a walk around the block to take a careful look at the buildings near the school, visits to nearby shops, to a factory, to a park, or to a museum. When given the right preparation and expectation, any such expedition may become a creative and rewarding experience.

On this page are drawings made by ten-year-olds during a visit to a Mennonite farm in Pennsylvania. Such sketches may be developed into more finished drawings or paintings at another time. When it is not feasible to carry sketching materials, someone might bring along a camera. However, just the sheer pleasure of carefully observing the scene, whether it is a clump of trees in a forest, or tenements huddled together in a crowded street, will serve as a vivid reminder of the experience.

Seven-year-olds have an opportunity to see an exhibit of contemporary art in their school. They may also sketch from nature; Adam is shown at work in a park nearby. From such diverse art experiences they learn how many possibilities for expression and enjoyment art holds.

A group of thirteen-year-olds on a class trip to The Guggenheim Museum look, sketch, and react to a painting by Kandinsky.

It is our desire to help children realize that art is an integral part of living, and that through it peoples of every culture and time have expressed their values and beliefs about life. For those we teach, art should be two things: a personal experience and opportunity to create and communicate; a key to deeper understanding and appreciation of the past and present through study of the art created by others.

Opportunities to see works of contemporary artists are always available in a big city. The children at our school may go the relatively short distance uptown to The Guggenheim Museum, or just across the street from the school to the outdoor sculpture exhibit at St. Mark's Church on the Bouwerie. Such experiences are a source of delight and a way to learn how artists interpret our own culture.

Children investigate one of the sculptures at the outdoor exhibit at St. Mark's Church. On the right is Pamela's drawing of the same work.

The children in the group that went across the street to see the St. Mark's Church sculpture exhibit ranged in age from six to nine. As we were leaving the school building, one of the nine-year-olds asked if he might take a pad and sketching pencil. The others, mostly younger, thought this was an excellent idea, and so everyone went to the outdoor sculpture exhibit with sketching supplies.

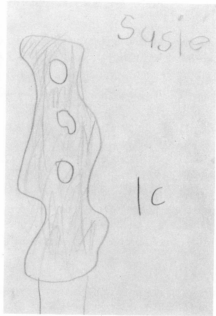

Here are more photographs of the children enjoying the exhibit and some of the drawings they made. They were allowed to touch the works; they peeked through holes and moved in and around the forms. They were able to move far enough away to see the total work and then come close enough to look at details. For the six- and seven-year-olds this was the first opportunity to do such sketching on a trip, and they felt this was really something special. Those who more thoroughly enjoyed looking did not feel they had to draw, though most did some sketching before the time was up.

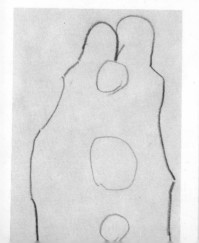

A trip requires careful planning, whether it is simply a walk around the block, or involves hours of travel. Knowing the class, the teacher can gauge the maximum amount of time the particular children are able to concentrate and remain involved. This length of time should be cut down by about a third, for experiences outside of the school building take a little more energy partially due to the added excitement of a new or different experience. When children become overly tired, time is wasted and nothing is gained. Sometimes it may be possible to break up a long trip by having a lunch and free-play period; this allows time for jumping and running about out-of-doors if the trip destination is near a park. During lunch they have a chance to joke and relax. Then they are ready to become involved once again in the topic at hand.

When school trips are handled wisely, children remember the experience with pleasure. They have been beautifully introduced to a new experience — an introduction which only barely scratches the surface of what is available. This is especially true of some of our big museums. The children are inspired to return again and again, bringing parents, siblings, friends. It becomes a part of them — a habit, and a joy.

Ten-year-olds are engrossed in a lecture on knights in armor.

Betsy carefully sketched a busy street in a small town.

If we believe that art should be part of the natural flow of experiences children have, then it follows that the classroom teacher as well as the art teacher (where one is available) ought to cooperate in planning the ways in which this might happen. For the most effective program coordination the teachers involved should be aware of the creative possibilities and also the pit falls. To further enhance this cooperative situation it is extremely important that parents are brought in on occasion for discussions of the growth and development of children. This will give parents a basis for understanding and responding to the art objects children bring home, and they will be better able to promote the child's interest in this subject. When parents understand the teacher's aims in planning and taking trips such as those described, they can be of valuable assistance either by occasionally providing needed transportation or by joining the class on trips as a helpful assistant. By taking children out of the classroom and into the world, teachers and parents can work together to bring to life what might otherwise remain words and pictures in a book.

117

Julie concentrating on a still life.

"ART IS A CAREER THAT PEOPLE LOVE."
— TEN-YEAR-OLD

TOWARD A
DEEPER INVOLVEMENT

The importance of having at least one art teacher in every elementary school is not to be under-estimated. The most capable classroom teacher cannot — and should not be expected to — offer art experiences in depth primarily because of the great number of other subjects that must be mastered and successfully taught. However, there is a shortage of art teachers, and until such time as the supply is equal to the demand, the best possible course for the present must be sought. It is incumbent upon those in the field of art and art education to so inspire classroom teachers as to elevate the quality of art experiences in the classroom one-hundred fold!

There is no doubt in my mind that by improving the classroom teacher's preparation in art we will eventually improve the quality of classroom art experiences. In schools with "traveling" art teachers the classroom teacher still finds herself all but in charge of the art curriculum. In schools with full time art teachers, the children may still only have the benefit of visiting the art room once each week.

Beyond doubt, art is one of the most valuable means of expression and effective aids to learning in the curriculum, and there is much to be done to see that it is presented in the best possible way to children. Just how important it is to the maturing and learning process of every child must be recognized by all those responsible for his growth and development. It is up to art teachers and art educators to impart their own enthusiasm for art and understanding of what it can accomplish. They must work with parents, administrators, and classroom teachers, leading them toward a deeper understanding of the creative needs of children who are seeking answers to the riddles of today's world!

John Dewey, in *Art as Experience,* pointed out: "Communication is the process of creating participation, of making common what has been isolated and singular; and part of the miracle that it achieves is that, being communicated, the conveyance of meaning gives body and definiteness to the experience of the one who utters as well as to that of those who listen."

We see communication as the vital link with others, and we try to find ways in which children can interact with each other in a positive way. For some, the non-verbal aspects of music, dance and the plastic arts prove of inestimable value. Ideas are played with and become meaningful through contact with the materials; soon communication is possible on many levels and the pleasure is hard to contain! In the average school situation many children come to us relatively free, full of enthusiasm, joyous about life, and open to creative experiences. Somehow we put them into a harness. We dim this spark of life quickly; the creative child upsets class routine so he must be tamed. And soon enough he knows this, or, what is worse, he may suffer abuses from teachers and peers which are hard to take. His psyche suffers, but the room is quiet and nothing is going on at all. Untold numbers of children, having been clobbered into silence by the so-called educative process, are numbed into nothingness, learning only by rote and not really caring at all. Teachers are generally aware of individual differences in children's academic abilities; it is also important to realize and respect the individual differences in the capacity for creativity and to help children understand them as well.

These five drawings (moving from left to right) were produced by children ages six, seven, eight, nine, and ten.

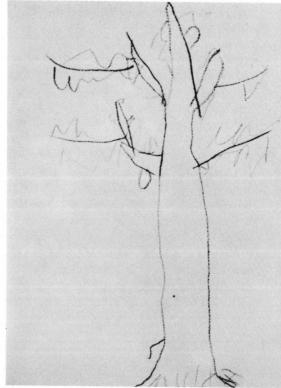

In art, no two children should be expected to respond in exactly the same way. In fact, the many differences in drawing and painting help everyone to appreciate the individual ways of responding to similar experiences. Children learn to evaluate their work, they compare what they did the previous week with what was

accomplished today, they try new ways, new ideas, they repeat a theme or a technique to improve, and in their seeking for ways to express what matters most they develop a personal style that is uniquely theirs. They remain open to new experiences, gathering each one within themselves and all of these combined create a way of thinking, of looking, and of responding to their environment.

The act of using art materials does not make children artists — just as using science materials will not make them scientists. But the opportunity to explore with these materials does allow children to make their own discoveries. If we tell them how to do everything, if we answer every question completely or imply there's only one "correct" answer, then there is nothing left for the child to do and very little challenge to do anything. By exploring on his own, with the teacher at hand for guidance and for clues toward furthering his understanding, the child will learn how to solve problems for himself.

We never really know when a child will "bloom," will really come through understanding and knowing how to think for himself in a variety of areas of learning. But we can help by offering the kind of atmosphere in which learning can take place. The things we do and the things we say count so much more than we realize!

Betsy's drawing of the coffee pot.

In *Creative Power,* Hughes Mearns noted: "Good teaching is not solely the business of instructing; it is also the art of influencing another. Primarily it is the job of uncovering and enlarging native gifts of insight, feeling, and thinking." We influence children by the tone we help to set in a room, by the kinds of questions we ask, and by the ability we have to accept and appreciate the range of differences that children exhibit in their responses.

The teachers who rigidly stick to the "how-to" suggestions that appear in some books and periodicals even in these enlightened times handicap and limit themselves as well as the learning opportunities and development of their children. Children accustomed to such structured nonthinking experiences at first do not know how to respond to the teacher who offers them freedom to make their own decisions. They seem to be waiting for the one-two-three steps to which they have been accustomed. No one makes a move to start on his own. It is as though they can't believe that such an opportunity is real or possible. Teachers need to lead such children gently toward each new art experience. As they realize that they are free to explore and experiment, to think about their own special way of working, and to use the materials as they desire, they will become involved and find a constructive outlet for ideas.

As a child grows, the effective teacher can judge the progress he has made in the time she has known him. If he has only crawled ahead a little and she knows he has been trying, then even this is a sign of achievement. Progress is not always spectacular, but it should be as great as possible at any given stage. Techniques for inspiring intellectual growth and development are as numerous as the differences in each of us. The inspiration, motivation, or stimulus that works in a given situation is the right one at that time and place. It is not a rigid formula to be followed ever after. There are many "right" answers to problems in art, and different paths of thought that will lead to major solutions. An atmosphere that encourages this kind of problem solving in a variety of subject areas is open to new ideas in an on-going and open-ended learning experience. This kind of inter-action adds fuel to the fire of learning. Sometimes a step-by-step method is best, other times an all-jumbled-up method is right, sometimes a head-on or upside-down approach works best. There is no one formula for excellent teaching and high-level learning.

In a dynamic society, change is the key. No matter what our field of specialization, we have the freedom to expand and explore within an over-all framework that remains flexible. We must offer children this same kind of opportunity. We need a youthful outlook backed by mature experience — the only magic formula there is.

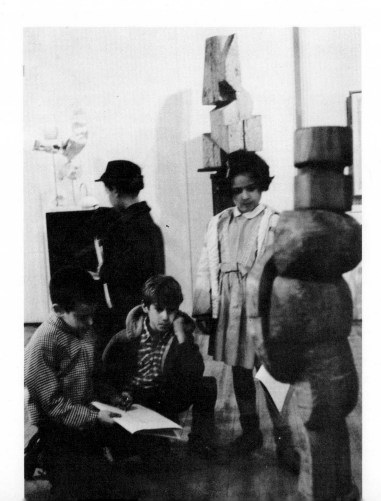

Each experience with art should offer a special adventure for a child. The blank paper offers a landing place; a child can quickly "write" upon it, cover up and write again, or he can slowly build up areas, moving on as he needs to find another place for more action.

This much we can observe: each child works from his own base as he tackles the job at hand. Some complete the job quickly, moving on to the next, and the next. Others, working with great detail can devote major attention to one drawing or painting, showing a sincere absorption in the process. Both care — or don't care — about the finished product at one time or another. It does not often seem to depend upon how much time was spent in the production. For many, the "doing" is more than enough reward. In fact, such children seeing their work on display are startled — some do not even recall it as their own, and some are embarrassed. But for those in need of ego-building, praise of their work is a superb experience and has a profound effect above and beyond the immediate moment. Seeing his work on display can be heartwarming to a child and may be the only "light" on an otherwise dim horizon at that moment. I remember Jimmy's mother coming to me so pleased to see one of his drawings on exhibit; she had just seen his teacher and confirmed her suspicion that he had fallen down on his academic work. We agreed that, building on his moderate success in art, we'd try to work with him toward achieving on a higher level in other areas as well.

The world encompasses many things. Eight-year-olds reflect in their drawings two important influences on their lives — space exploration and the Beatles.

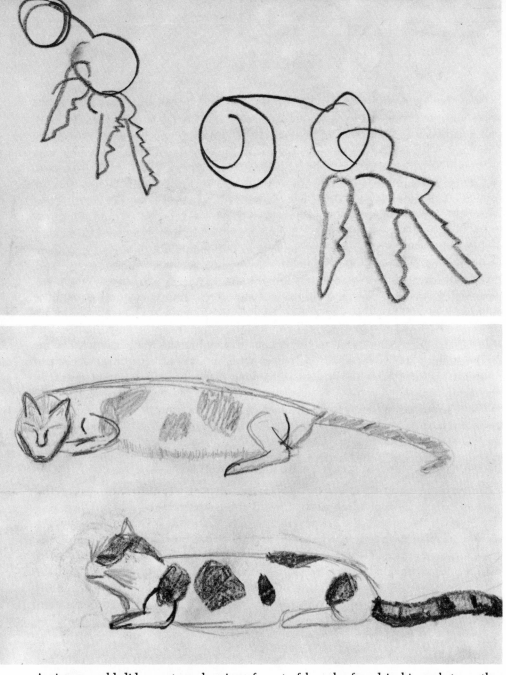

A nine-year-old did a contour drawing of a set of keys he found in his pocket; another sketched her cat in different moods.

Children feel free to talk, sometimes almost describing what they do as they work, at other times chatting about something quite different and unconnected, as though involved in two different things at the same time. They ask profound questions with an air of utter simplicity, assuming that you, as an adult, can pop up with easy answers — and if not, why not? Sometimes they are merely waiting for you to turn the question back at them. They are ready to answer their own questions with gusto and the confidence of youth!

In his book *On Knowing*, Jerome Bruner states: "Art helps us connect experiences and the experience of art nourishes itself. . . . Having sensed connectedness one is impelled to seek more of it." Sensing relationships, seeing connections, rearranging evidence to achieve new insights, all these lead to a fusion of symbol and imagery which allows us to achieve some level of creativity. The sudden awareness of connections can be as exciting for an adult as it is for a child; the opportunity to help others move toward discovery is a major reward for a teacher. Part of our work with children involves helping them to think about an experience, ask questions, learn to listen as others speak, and have the actual experience. Teaching and learning is not just all talk and no action! But T. S. Eliot reminds us, in *Four Quartets*, that it is possible to "have the experience and miss the meaning." And this is at the heart of our concern. One might pile up tons of experiences which are meaningless, that use our most precious commodity — time — but add nothing to enhance life.

Let us consider, for a moment, the people involved in the learning situation. In the beginning there is the child. He comes with certain real and imaginary experiences; he is involved with constantly changing and growing relationships to self, peers, adults.

The teacher has a concept of self, each child has a concept of "teacher." The teacher relates to each one, and to the class as a whole. She calls forth different aspects of self, depending upon the needs of those with whom she is interacting at the moment. She helps children to develop an awareness of self, move toward making connections with others, to and with life.

Martin Buber said: "To live in freedom is a personal responsibility." And the teacher tries to help children move toward this responsibility. The art teacher's role involves the school, the art program, and her place as a person in the larger society, in relation to art, to education, and therefore, to life. She, too, must become aware of personal responsibility. But most of all, as "teacher" she is involved with children who look to her for guidance, sharing what she knows and shedding light on paths to be taken, pointing out new ways of becoming involved which allow the students to eventually surpass the teacher. For in an atmosphere conducive to "supplying conditions for growth," (Dewey) this will surely happen.

The experience of teaching goes beyond the active or passive involvement between teacher, student, subject. It is encompassed by life — and the dynamic forces in life act and interact in their own way on each individual. To function effectively under these circumstances, we seek a way to function in a positive fashion with others. This seems automatic, but is it really? The capacity for being and becoming varies greatly, leading to the diversity which is basic to our society. Diversity implies a breadth of differences acceptable within our social structure. Each child is guided into life and on toward living, surrounded by diversity. At the same time he is aware of something else — conformity. For he is constantly reminded about the "right way" to do certain things. Between these opposites a way must be found that requires only the conformity that is good and necessary, and encourages a healthy diversity. Perhaps failing to find the "way" accounts for

126

the many who "have the experience but miss the meaning" and fall by the wayside. What Bruner in *The Process of Education* has called " . . . the courageous leap to a tentative conclusion . . ." can take place in an atmosphere that allows open-ended thinking. Degrees of allowable diversity are tempered by the kind of activity involved, by the flexibility of the group, the capacity of the teacher and her ability to allow children the pleasure of seeking new answers to old questions. Such an atmosphere may be a breath of fresh air to some, create a fear of the unknown in others, and lead to chaotic responses from still others who feel the need to burst forth, and who have little experience in containing themselves when offered the opportunity to expand. Therefore, it must be handled carefully, more circumscribed at first, and then developed so that all the children will be able to function effectively, making creative use of the freedom to be themselves, learn, and learn to think.

A still life by a child of six, and a stone fence that threads among the trees painted by a thirteen-year-old.

"We've been there before."
"We've seen that before."
"We've done that before."

How often teachers hear children responding this way. We are reminded of the attitude that "having done something once is more than enough." Children reflecting this notion seem to be always seeking newness, ready to discard a single experience because it is no longer new. This is learned from adults; we have our own cult of "newness" which children easily emulate. This is not to say that new things as well as new experiences have no meaning or value. The challenge lies in seeking what is new, but not at the expense of those experiences often revisited that may continue to enrich our lives.

We are working in a dynamic field. New ideas are constantly being brought forth to question and challenge programs and methods currently in use. Philosophies come and go. Though children are eventually affected by major changes in curriculum and methods, we need to continue to rely on common sense along with experience. Of course we must be aware of the research and developments that teach us more about children and about art, but we also need the confidence and courage to question and to challenge. In our profession, as in everything else, simply because something is "new" does not automatically mean it is better. Openness, flexibility, awareness should be key words for every one of us. We are in the majority of followers, the leaders are few, as is usually the case. Yet we must remember that these leaders are not "gods," and, therefore, not omniscient. Unless we are able to evaluate and interpret what they say, we follow blindly. If the broad concepts, generally stated, seem to be theoretically sound, we, as the interpreters, must learn to apply them in rooms full of lively children; this is where the action is, where we as art teachers either sink or soar, and where children either sink or soar in their learning.

Children respond to art on many levels. It is one of the few areas in the curriculum where feelings are allowed to show, where the pleasurable aspects of learning can take root and blossom, where each can truly respond in his own unique way to materials, and attempt to depict his own private ideas as he desires. Here, children sketch as a classmate poses.

Children's experiences in drawing and painting have been presented here as a temptation to explore a few of the possibilities available with simple supplies and an open heart. When we present art materials to children, we need to learn that they have many excellent ideas, and there are times when we get in the way of allowing children the pleasure of using their own ideas, sharing them with us and with their peers. We need to guide, but not rigidly direct. Teachers who paint or draw at home or in school before children arrive in the morning, or after they leave in the afternoon, will understand the process and the problems and find themselves better able to present art media to children. There is no better way than having a continuing personal involvement with art.

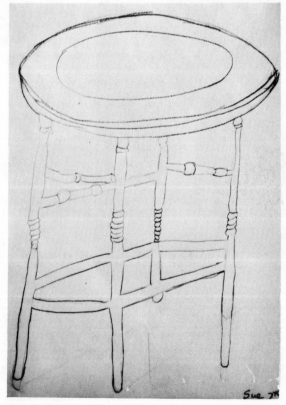

Through art the most humble objects, the most seemingly unimportant experiences, take on a life of their own. Here, Sue, age twelve, drew the high stool in the art room.

130

Discovery, involvement, joy, and satisfaction await the child. The early experiences with art can offer these — and the challenge to move toward the greater discoveries ever greater maturity requires.

131

Every classroom, whatever the curriculum, is a laboratory for learning which ought to involve the teacher as well as the children. As we attempt to develop a personal philosophy we ought to be asking ourselves questions, conducting our own "self-investigation," our own attempt to find answers. What happens day by day? Can *we* make the kind of connection we expect of the children? What do the children think? What ideas do they present? What do they let us know about themselves? How do peers influence what happens? How much do the children influence what happens? How do they respond in drawing? In painting? What do they say with texture, color, light and dark — and with words? Intuition? Intellect? Imagination? What is their response to you, to the art room, to materials, to self, to other adults? What is their response to nature, the city, love, war, life? How do you respond? How do you make things count? What framework is best? How do you help to relate the inner world and the outer world? The eye, the hand, the heart?

Such earnest searching is a part of every teacher's responsibility to every child, every class. And there is always a bell, or clock, or calendar to remind us that time is running out. Will we ever feel that we have really accomplished all we had hoped to with any group of children in an hour or a year? Teaching involves love, and it involves life. It involves caring and responding. It involves knowing and understanding. It involves awareness. Where is a child when he comes into your room? And how far has he traveled into himself — and out into the world, when he leaves?